MAKING UNU

C000115127

MAKING UNUSUAL MINIATURES

GRAHAM SPALDING

GUILD OF MASTER CRAFTSMAN PUBLICATIONS LTD

First published 1989 by Guild of Master Craftsman Publications Ltd,
166 High Street, Lewes, East Sussex BN7 1XU

Reprinted 1993

© Graham Spalding 1989

ISBN 0946819 13 0

All rights reserved

No part of this publication may be reproduced, stored in a retrieval system, or transmitted in any form or by any means without prior permission of the copyright owner.

Designed by Peter Ward

Photoset by Parker Typesetting Service, Leicester

Printed and bound in Great Britain at
Hillman Printers (Frome) Ltd

ACKNOWLEDGEMENTS

I must thank the following people and organisations for their help in allowing me to sketch and measure the projects for this book:

D. Alston, Esq., for the Mendlesham Chair; the curator and staff of Colchester Museum for the Spinning Wheel; the principal and staff of Colchester School of Music for the Harp; the Goff Gallery, Long Melford, for the Drum Table; the staff at Prettygate Library.

I would also like to thank my wife and family for all their support and encouragement.

CONTENTS

NOTE ON SCALE

All the drawings in this volume are to the scale of one inch to the foot and can be traced and used for making the miniatures. The exception to this is the Snooker Table.

TIMBER

THE subject of timber for miniature-making is, as are so many things in miniature work, a matter of personal taste. But having said this, there are certain woods which are undoubtedly better than others. Most people who are at all interested in timber realise that there are two main categories: softwoods and hardwoods. You also hear people talking about deal, but there is no such timber. A 'deal' is a 9″ by 3″ piece of softwood, usually pine or fir.

Of the softwoods there is, in my opinion, only one suitable for miniatures and that is yew, a beautiful wood which is red when first cut but turns brown on exposure to air. It is fine-grained, works well and takes a fine finish. Balsa is not a softwood, but has no place in miniature work anyway, unless as padding or an infill, being far too soft.

This leaves the hardwoods, of which there are so many that I will only mention a few of the more popular ones. As a general rule, if the timber is not too coarse-grained, if it will take a good finish, and if it looks right, then use it!

SYCAMORE A pale, straight-grained wood, rather featureless, used in the past for kitchen utensils.

BOXWOOD Distinctive yellow colour, superb for turning and carving, takes detail well and is easy to finish. Hard to find now, but old rulers are probably the best source of supply for miniaturists.

ROSEWOOD Brown, through purple, to almost black, it is a very hard wood which turns and finishes well. A messy timber to actually work, but looks lovely when polished.

EBONY Strangely, not always pure black. Scarce and hard to find now, difficult to work, but takes a superb finish.

JELUTONG A creamy, straw-coloured wood, soft and easy to work and will take fine detail when worked with sharp tools.

SAPELE A mahogany-coloured wood often used as a mahogany substitute.

UTILE Very much like sapele but not quite so attractive; much used for plywood.

BEECH Pale brown in colour and has a distinctive flecked appearance when quarter sawn; works easily, takes a good finish. Much used in the furniture trade.

ASH White to pale cream and can have a very attractive grain. For miniature work it needs to be picked carefully as it can be difficult to finish.

RAMIN Almost white; fine, even texture; works well and is easily obtainable – a very useful timber.

HOLLY Greyish-white, featureless timber; hard, very close-grained and much favoured by miniaturists for carving as it will accept sharp detail.

WALNUT Grey-brown with almost black streaks; works easily and is noted for its excellent finish – one of my favourites.

CUBAN MAHOGANY The Rolls-Royce of mahoganies. Warm brown to red in colour, straight, close-grained, works superbly. Very hard to come by, so if you find some, keep it to yourself.

APPLE Pale pinkish-brown, difficult to dry as it splits easily; nice to work when dry, and finishes well.

OLIVEWOOD Pale brown to darker brown with black or grey markings; a very striking wood which is highly decorative, works well and takes an excellent finish. Needs care in selecting the prototype for use in a model.

AFRORMOSIA Yellow-brown to brown, sometimes mistaken for teak; has an interlocking grain and can be difficult to work.

CHERRY Pale pinkish-brown and like all the fruitwoods not easy to dry; works well and takes a good finish.

PEAR The same colour as cherry, but cherry darkens more when dry than pear. Not so easy to work due to twisting grain; takes a good finish.

WHITE OAK This is the common European oak. It has a very distinctive coarse grain and needs to be used carefully for miniature work or it can look out of scale; needs to be dry to work well.

TEAK Uniform golden-brown; not easy to work and usually too coarse-grained to be much use in miniature work. Hard to glue, but for all that, a beautiful timber.

LIME This is the wood that Americans call basswood. Pale, almost white, wood that darkens on exposure; nice straight grain. All-time favourite for carving – a very useful wood.

OBECHE Next to balsa, the lightest hardwood. Pale straw-yellow colour with natural sheen; fairly easy to work with sharp tools; useful.

The best source of supply usually suggested for miniaturists is old furniture, and this is indeed so, as long as you know your timber and what you are getting. As a rule, whatever you get from old furniture, there is far too much of it. I have some lovely Cuban mahogany taken from an old bed, but I shall never manage to use a half of it. A strong case can be made for drying some of your own timber, especially some of the fruitwoods. Miniaturists normally use so little timber that it really is worth drying some small branches for yourself.

For more exotic woods you can usually find a supplier somewhere in the district who will let you have a small quantity, or you can look in one of the woodworking magazines which will give the names of lots of mail-order firms.

TOOLS AND TIPS

IT IS almost compulsory to start a book of this nature with a chapter on the tools required to make miniatures. Everyone has heard of 'Bert' who does the most incredible things with old wooden cotton reels and his great-grandfather's penknife, and long may he prosper, but for every Bert there are considerably more of us lesser mortals who find that the right tool for the right job makes things easier and helps to retain the pleasure in what we are doing.

This does not mean that there is only one tool for each job, as every task has a number of possible solutions, and in the main the right tool is the one you feel happiest with. For this reason I am not going to give you a list of the tools you need to make miniatures. It is far better to have a limited number of tools that you are confident with, and can use well, than to have a box full, some of whose names you may not even know. (I have a great number of tools, collected over 40 years of model-making, and many of them rarely see the light of day.)

THE BASIC TOOLS

Let us consider the tasks to be undertaken and the basic tools needed. The first step in any project is to prepare the wood. The essential thing here is a means of measuring. There are lots of sophisticated measuring devices, but a plain, simple 6- or 12-inch steel ruler will do very well to start with. That, coupled with a sharp pencil, will probably take care of ninety per cent of all your measuring.

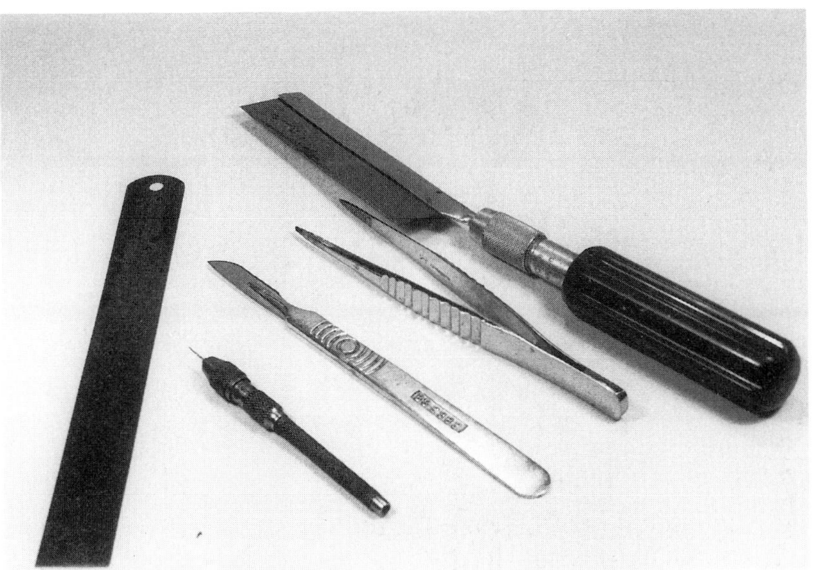

PHOTOGRAPH 1
Left to right: steel ruler; small drill; scalpel; tweezers; razor saw.

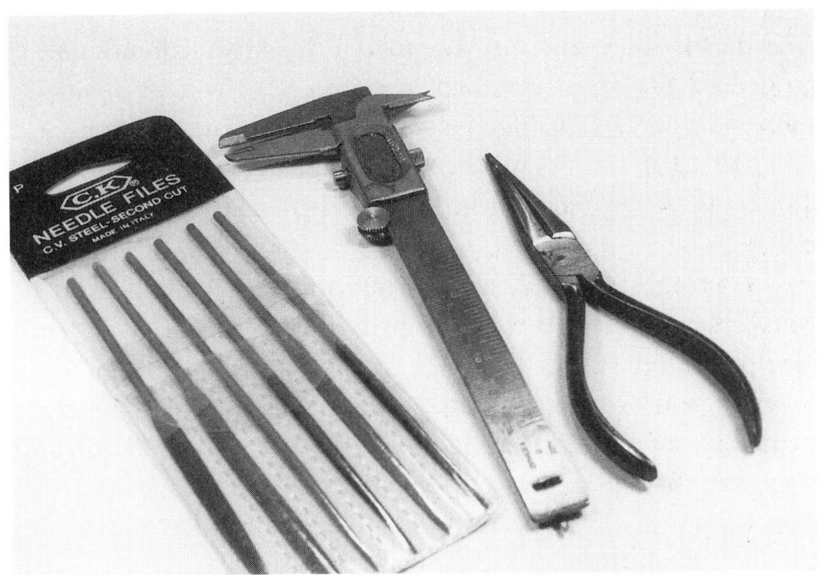

PHOTOGRAPH 2
Left to right: needle files; measuring calipers; small pliers.

The next step is to cut the wood to size. The saw is our main ally in this step. Don't knock the handsaw – they used to build very big wooden ships with nothing else! You can still prepare all your timber requirements with a good sharp handsaw – it will take longer, that's all. With DIY shops now carrying a wide range of wooden mouldings, it is sometimes unnecessary to do much in the way of heavy preparation. However, if you are determined to build your

PHOTOGRAPH 3
Left to right: junior hacksaw; small plane; tenon saw.

Mendlesham Chair from the branch of a tree, you are going to need a bit of power to help out. There is a tremendous range of power saws on the market for miniature work, and if I had to make do with only one, it would be my small bandsaw. Apart from large planks, I prepare all my timber on it.

Having sawn the timber roughly to size, you need to finish it, and for this there is little to beat a hand plane and sandpaper.

To work the wood into the finished product, there are probably half a dozen special tools for every single action and you will discover from experience the one or two that suit you best, but do try a number 3 scalpel holder and blade, better I think than all the fancy craft knives. A small bench hook is very useful, together with a razor saw.

Some of the pieces in this book do call for the use of a lathe. Any of the small lathes on the market will suffice, and an add-on to a drill is quite adequate, as you will find that it will extend enormously the range of objects you can tackle.

I shall be surprised if you do not find that you end up with just a few tools that you use most of the time. With all tools, please remember the motto my grandfather had in letters a foot high along the wall of his workshop: KEEP YOUR HANDS BEHIND THE CUTTING EDGE.

USEFUL DEVICES TO MAKE

There are four small items which you can make which you will find invaluable for miniature work. The first of these is a device for cramping up table tops (Photograph 4) or for that matter anything else which needs to be held closely together, on the flat, while the glue dries. The photograph is self-explanatory, and the size is not really very important as long as it is big enough to take a reasonably-sized table top. The one in the picture is made of a spare length of 6″ wide melamine-faced chipboard shelving, but any piece of smooth timber or chipboard will do, so long as it is about 6″ wide and at least 9″ long.

To either side of the short way, glue and screw two pieces of $\frac{1}{2}$″ square timber – this is the only really important part of the job. *Do make sure that these two pieces are parallel to each other.* Why? Because the whole thing works on the principle of folding wedges, and if the two fixed runners are not parallel, things will not glue up square!

The last part of the job is to make the folding wedges. For this you will need a piece of timber $\frac{1}{2}$″ thick by $1\frac{1}{2}$″ and approximately 8″ long. Starting $\frac{1}{8}$″ in, at either end, draw a

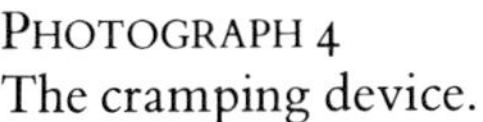
PHOTOGRAPH 4
The cramping device.

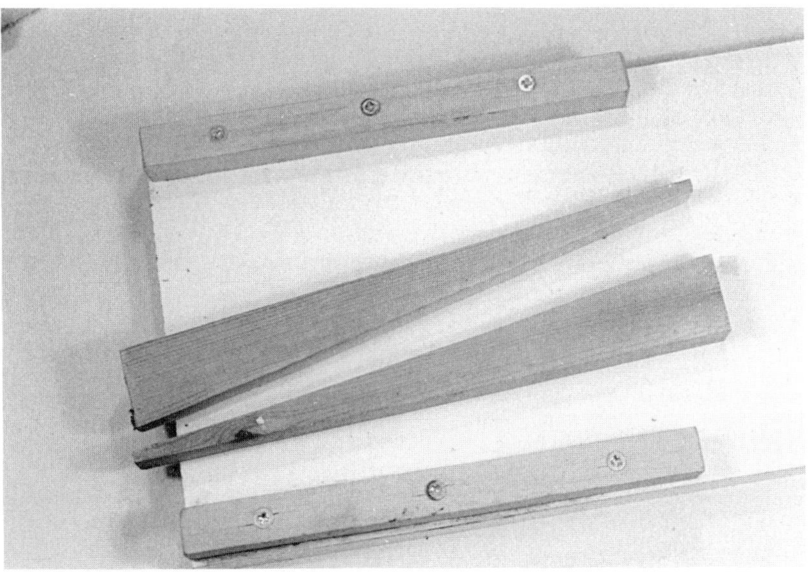

diagonal line the length of the wood and cut along this line. You should end up with two long triangular wedges, as in the photograph. Clean up the sawn edges, and you are all set to use your cramp.

The second little tool that I suggest you make is a draw plate, Photograph 5. This you will find invaluable, and in almost constant use for making dowels for joining parts of furniture together, and for all kinds of location purposes. You can, of course, use cocktail sticks for this purpose, and indeed wherever possible do make use of these ready-made dowels, but you will find that there are occasions when they are just too big and it is very handy to be able to produce your own dowels as fine as you like.

The draw plate in the photograph is made from a piece of 24 gauge mild steel plate, size 3″ × 2″. It is bent at right angles to make it easier to hold, and drilled in easy stages from number 47 drill, which is the one for cocktail sticks, to number 57. Do not worry if you are mystified by '24 gauge mild steel' or are unable to find any easily. Use a pressed-steel shelf bracket that you can buy from any DIY shop for about 25p – it will work just as well. Drill the holes for the size of dowels you need, and all you have to do is push your dowel stock through the holes to the size you require.

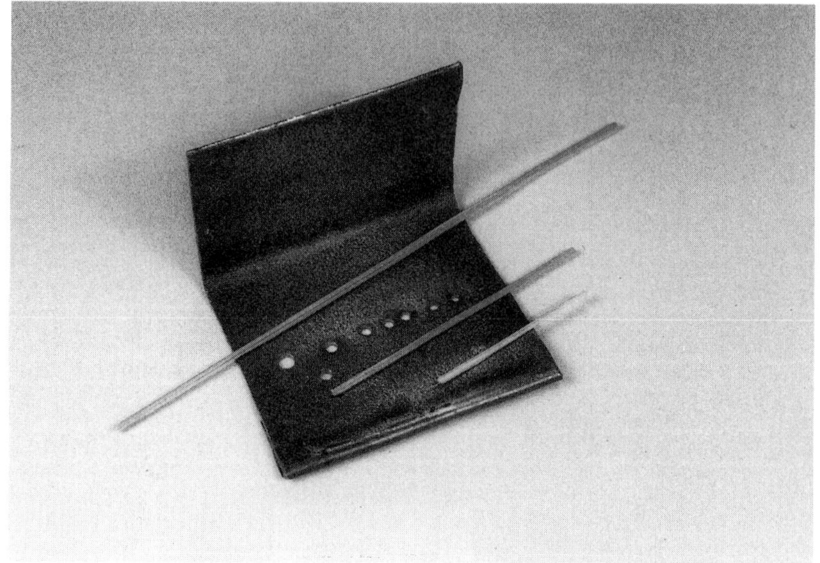

PHOTOGRAPH 5
The draw plate.

Having mentioned cocktail sticks, I should add that I do not think they are the best thing to make the finer dowels from, and I prefer to use bamboo. No problem about raw material here – all you need is a small section of garden cane, cut between joints. You will find that it splits easily with a knife, and you can split it until it is near enough to go through your draw plate. It should do so easily, especially if you give it a twist as you push. If your raw material is a bit too thick, use a pair of pliers to grip and pull it through. You can also get the raw material from any shop that sells barbecue equipment, where it is stocked as 'disposable kebab skewers'.

The final two items are both very simple, but useful, and easily made. Photograph 6 shows them clearly and is also almost self-explanatory. The first is a small bench saddle, which not only saves space but is much easier to use with the small pieces of wood we are normally concerned with. The second is a piece of sandpaper stuck to a small 'D' section piece of timber, and is absolutely invaluable for sanding and cleaning up inside curves.

You will find these four little tools very useful and well worth the effort of making.

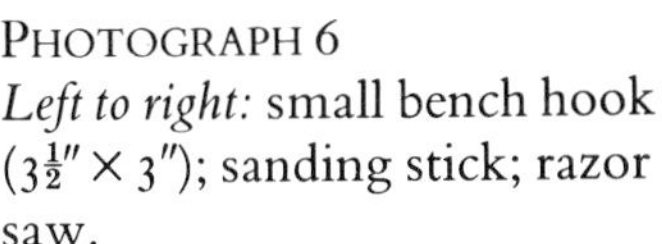

PHOTOGRAPH 6
Left to right: small bench hook ($3\frac{1}{2}'' \times 3''$); sanding stick; razor saw.

GLUES

In writing the notes to the projects I have tried to put in as many little tips as I can, but one other thing I would like to mention here is glue.

There are such a bewildering number of glues on the market that you would have to be very hard to please if you couldn't find one you liked. Indeed, there are so many that a recap may help. The old, so-called 'animal' glues that had to be heated are now fairly difficult to find, and I doubt if many joiner's shops still have a pot continually on the go, though it is still the best glue for veneering. Modern glue guns are, I suppose, the equivalent, but not a lot of use to miniaturists. The PVA (polyvinyl acetate adhesive) type is a good basic wood glue, my favourite being Evostik Resin W wood glue. You do have to remember to wipe off the surplus, particularly if you want to add stain after construction. The urea formaldehyde resin glues, such as Aerolite 306, are of little use to the miniaturist unless a waterproof bond is required. Apart from the white glues there are two others I use. One is a rapid hardening epoxy glue – Araldite Rapid – and the other is Copydex for gluing fabric. I am not very fond of the cyanoacrylates or so-called 'super glues', perhaps because they never seem to work for me. (I have no connection with any of the firms which make the above glues, they are just the ones that I like to use.)

TAPE

There are two other products that are vital when making miniatures. One is ordinary masking tape – not for masking, but for holding parts in place while the glue dries. The other is double-sided tape, which is also invaluable for holding small pieces in place.

FINISHING

I have written very little about finishing the models. This is because I like to finish the majority of mine with a wax polish, which is in effect the same as leaving them natural, and there is not a lot you *can* say about that!

SCALE

One final point before we get on to the projects: all the drawings (except the Snooker Table) are full size to a scale of 1 inch to the foot. For this reason there are very few dimensions marked on them. I was taught in imperial, and in spite of all the years I have had to work in metric, I still *think* in imperial. I hope that people younger than myself will have a go at some of the projects, and as there are no sizes marked on them you can take them off the drawings just as you like and use whichever suits you best.

OAK REFECTORY TABLE AND BENCHES

THE table and benches have been designed to be made from a single piece of wood 3′6″ long by 1⅛″ wide and $\frac{3}{16}$″ thick, or several smaller pieces. This means that if you do not yet have a means of reducing timber yourself, you should be able to find something roughly the right size in a DIY shop.

The timber itself can be any suitable wood you fancy.

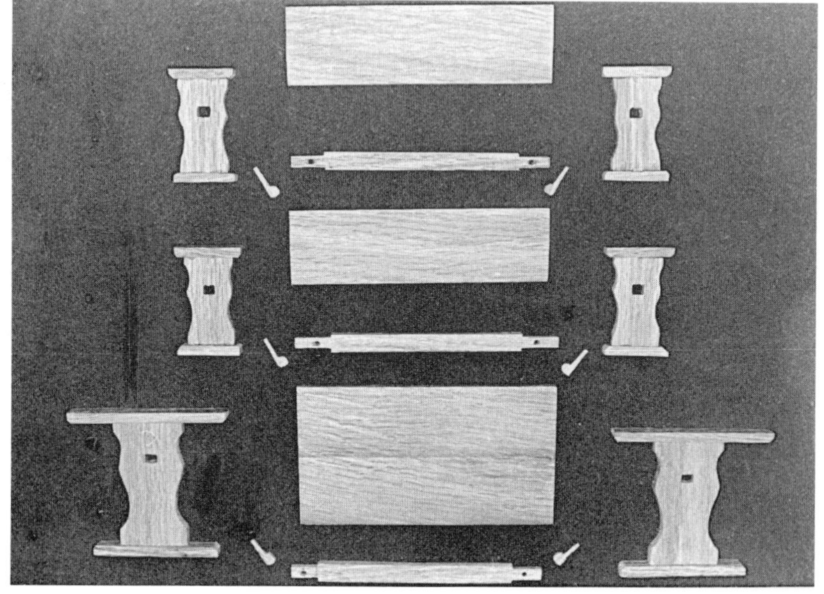

PHOTOGRAPH 1. The parts of the table and benches.

The pieces illustrated were made from English oak, but maybe a closer-grained timber would be more appropriate, such as ramin or beech. The next task, after selecting the wood, is to cut to length sufficient pieces to make all the separate parts. Photograph 1 shows the pieces. Remember that you will have to cut some of the pieces into narrower widths for the rails, so you do not need a separate length for each rail. Two pieces will have to be joined together to form the table top, and here you will need dowels and the cramping device (see page 7) for the first time. Of course if you have managed to find a piece of wood of the right width, you can make the top all in one. Although it is easier, it does not look right, so we will assume that you are going to be brave and tackle the joint.

TABLE TOP

With a very sharp pencil draw a centre line along the $\frac{3}{16}''$ edge of each of two pieces of wood of the correct length. The easy way to do this is to hold the pencil firmly between the first finger and thumb, and resting on the second finger. Using

PHOTOGRAPH 2. Drawing the centre line.

the second finger as a gauge, draw the line. It does not sound very easy? Well, Photograph 1 shows exactly how it is done, and with a little practice you will be surprised at how accurate a method it can be. With the lines drawn, take a small drill and make a number of holes along the line on one of the pieces of timber. Three is all I made in mine. Insert a short length of dowel with a touch of glue in each hole, then hold the two pieces of timber together, drilled and marked edges towards you. Mark on the line on the undrilled edge the position of the dowels, and drill those holes. For this type of drilling I find it easiest to use a small drill held in a pin vice and turned by fingers, as in Photograph 3. Putting the pieces together should be quite straightforward as long as you have marked and drilled the second set of holes accurately. If they do not quite meet, do not worry. Simply enlarge the holes slightly, and all will be well. Apply some glue to the edges and cramp up the top in the cramping device (see page 7). One final tip: a little wax polish under the top will stop any excess glue adhering to the wrong places.

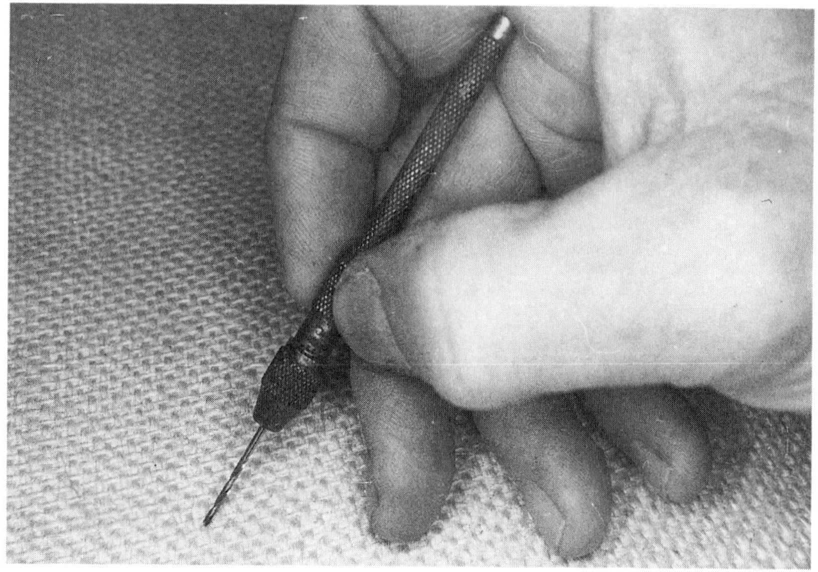

PHOTOGRAPH 3. Small drill held in pin vice.

TABLE AND BENCH ENDS

Now is the time to cut out the shaped table and bench ends. You can take the shape straight from Figures 3 and 4, either by tracing, or by making a cardboard templet and marking them from that. The cutting is probably easiest done with a fret saw. Initially, drill the hole for the bottom rail with a suitably-sized drill and open up to the square shape with a small file.

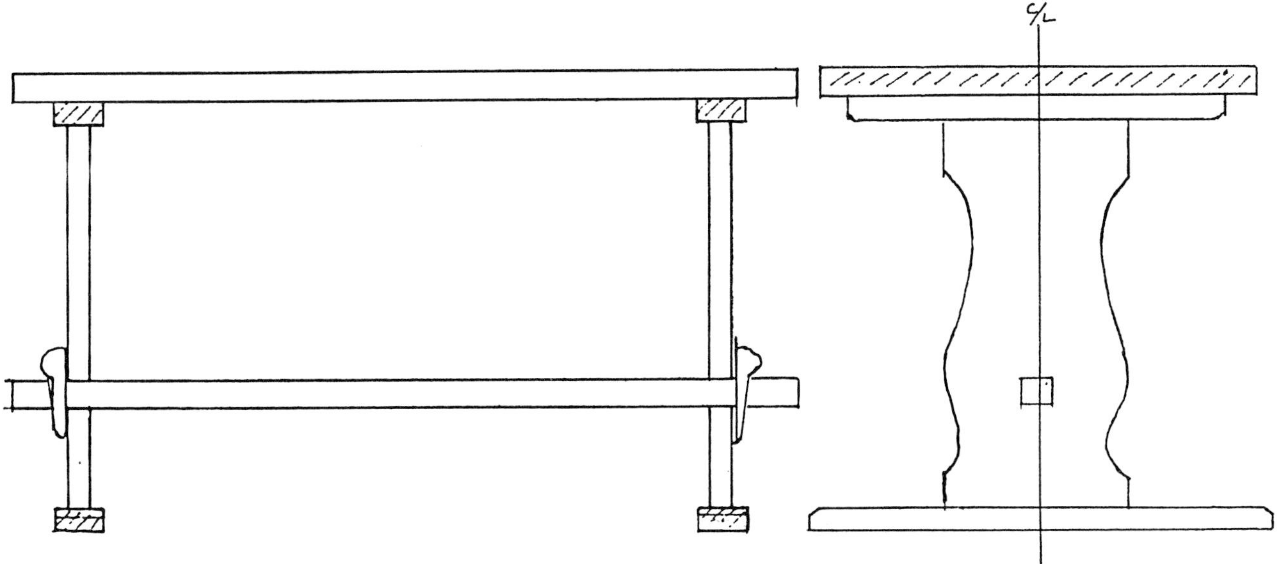

FIGURE 1. The side of the table.

FIGURE 3. The end of the table.

All timber $1\frac{1}{2}''$ scale, widths as indicated.

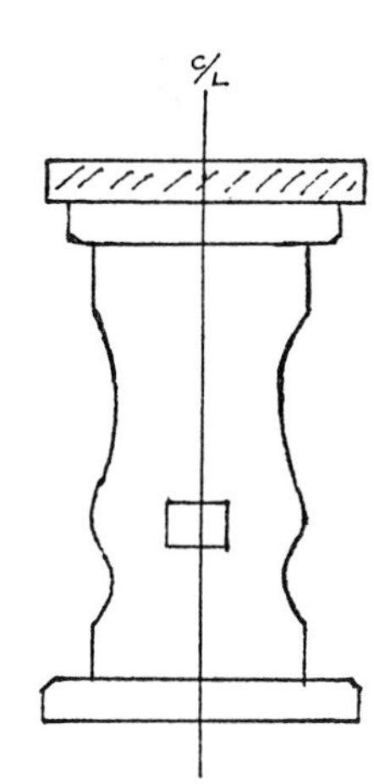

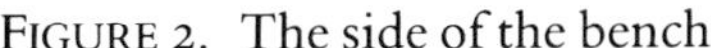

FIGURE 2. The side of the bench.

FIGURE 4. The end of the bench.

While you have the fret saw out, cut all the rest of the rails to the right length. You will note that they are all the same width and thickness.

RAILS

The long bottom rails of both the table and benches are probably the most outstanding part of these pieces of furniture and as such need to be well made. This is not difficult, it just needs a bit of time and patience. Starting with the table, take one of the pieces of wood cut to size for the bottom rail. On one end either cut or file the shoulders until it is a nice tight fit in the hole in the table end, and sticks through far enough to get the peg in, see Figure 5. Mark and drill a small hole for the pin. This needs to appear square, and the best way to do this is to replace the drill in the hole, and while turning it, to move it backwards and forwards to form an angle of 45 degrees both ways. This will elongate the hole and allow you to insert a rectangular pin.

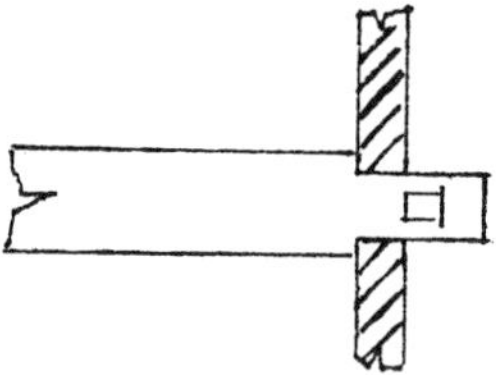

FIGURE 5. Detail of end of bottom rails, the same for table and benches.

To make the pin, start with a small piece of wood of the right size and cut a V notch in the top surface two-thirds of the way along. Taper the long side, round off the small end, then insert the pin in the ready made hole to make sure it fits (see Figure 6). I reckon if I can achieve a 50 per cent success rate for making pins I am doing well. Another five tusk tenon joints need to be made in the same way.

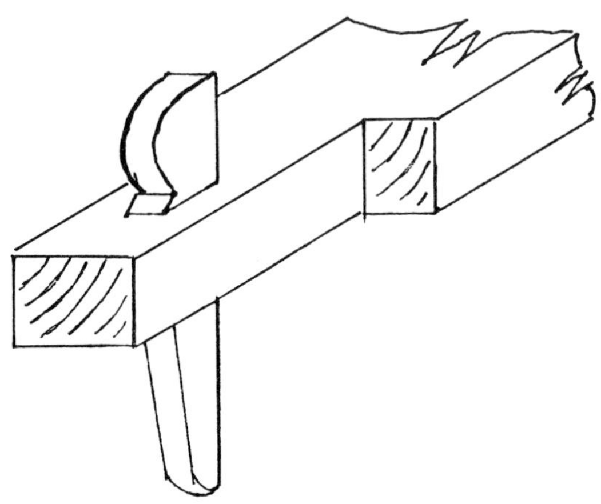

FIGURE 6. Detail of tusk tenon joint (not to scale).

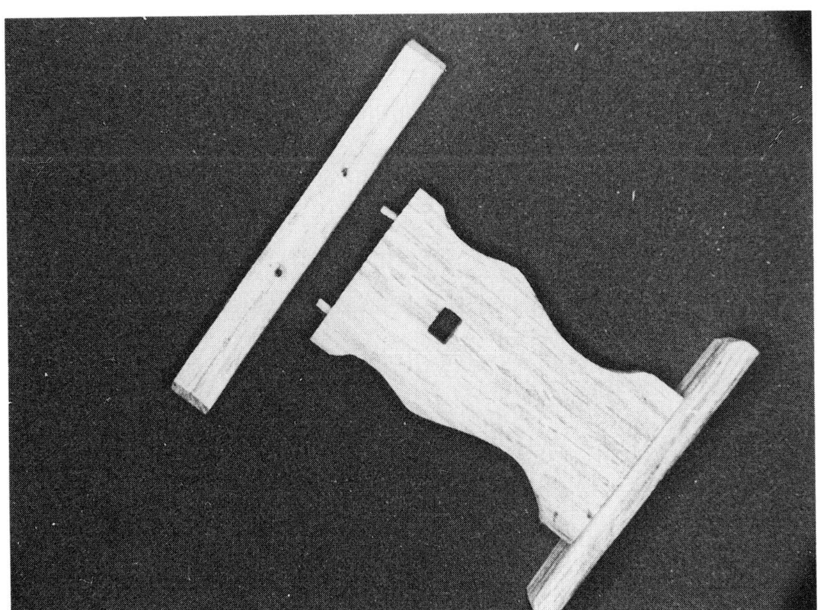

PHOTOGRAPH 4. Assembling the ends.

Having made all the bottom rails and checked that they fit the holes in the ends properly, you can now fix the head and foot rails, see Figures 3 and 4. This is a repeat of the drilling and dowelling operation to joint the table top and is quite simple, if time-consuming. Photograph 4 shows how it looks. This is the time to stain all the separate pieces, if you wish.

ASSEMBLY

Now for the final construction. You should have a collection of pieces looking like those in Photograph 1. Start by putting the ends together with the bottom rails, and inserting the pins. Next, mark, drill and glue on the table top and bench seats, again using dowels to locate and secure. One last tip: do drill the locating pin holes in the top *carefully* at this late stage. It is very frustrating, to say the least, to produce a neat little hole in a top!

PHOTOGRAPH 5. The complete table and benches.

Final finishing is to your taste, but I think a good wax polish looks well. That is how the ones illustrated (Photograph 5) are finished.

CORNER GUN CUPBOARD

IN AN age when sporting guns were used for sport, and not for holding up banks, and the rules for keeping them were less strict, it was quite commonplace for the study to contain a gun cupboard. The subject of this model is shown in the drawing with a Queen Anne-style head to the door, and in the photographs without one. The same drawings can be used to produce an ordinary corner cupboard, in which case I would suggest that it is made an inch shorter. It is only made to this height in order to accept the guns. I chose walnut for this model, as it looks well and is easy to work.

BODY OF CUPBOARD

Start with the front corner uprights. The easy way to make these is to cut a square section to the largest dimension taken from Figs. 1 & 2. That means a piece of wood $\frac{1}{2}''$ wide, $\frac{1}{4}''$ deep and just over 4″ long. Carefully plane the two flats on the corner to form the angles to the front and the door recess (Figure 2). On one back corner, form a rebate to accept the plywood sides. Don't forget that this rebate will need to be handed. (I think it is quite in order to use plywood for the sides as it is, after all, a corner cupboard, and they will not be seen except inside the cupboard, and there they can be stained.) The back corner needs a piece of timber about $\frac{3}{8}''$ square, with one corner planed off to form a triangle. That leaves the base to be cut out and a rebate, or round, moulded on the leading edge. Even the smallest portable drill can be adapted to form a mini-router, and with a ball-shaped cutter will put an excellent moulding on the edge. Photograph 1 shows all the pieces ready for assembly, with dowels and their sockets also visible.

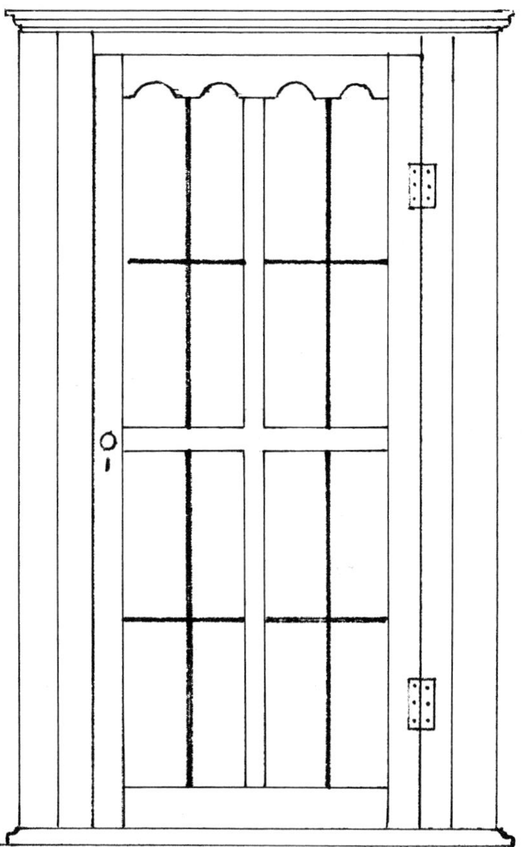

FIGURE 1. Front elevation.

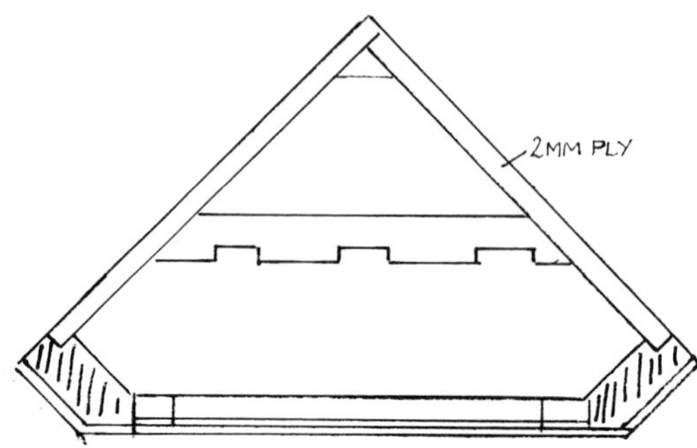

FIGURE 2. Plan of cupboard.

You can now put the cupboard together. This is quite a tricky operation and you may find it easier to do in stages. The first step is to glue the plywood sides into the rebates made for them in the front corners and put the whole thing aside to dry. Next, fix the front corners to the base and the back support between the sides. As the cupboard is relatively tall, it pays to fix the corner pieces to the base with dowels, likewise the back support. Drill and fix the dowels in the bases of the uprights first, then carefully mark the cupboard

PHOTOGRAPH 1. The main parts ready for assembly.

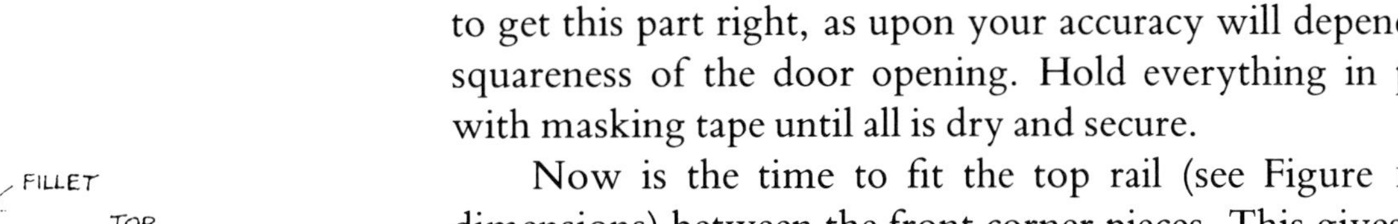

base before drilling the holes. It is worth taking a bit of time to get this part right, as upon your accuracy will depend the squareness of the door opening. Hold everything in place with masking tape until all is dry and secure.

Now is the time to fit the top rail (see Figure 1 for dimensions) between the front corner pieces. This gives you a further chance to make sure that all is as square as possible. When the rail is glued in place, cut and fit the top, which again can be plywood. This leaves the pediment moulding to be made and fitted.

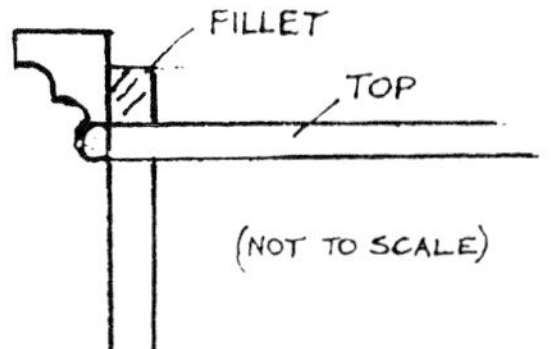

FIGURE 3. Detail of pediment.

The moulding does not have to follow the one in Figure 3, but can be a much simpler affair. Also, if you cannot rig up a drill as a router you can use a small, purpose-made scratch block, or even run it over a finely set circular-saw blade. If you still don't fancy the task, well, you can always buy a moulding from a model shop. Finally, mitre the moulding and glue it in place. Photograph 2 shows the cupboard assembled so far, with the shelf in place (see page 22). The shelf can be fitted at this stage, or at the end.

DOOR

This brings us to the door. Now there are two ways to make the door: the first is to make it properly, as a cabinet maker

PHOTOGRAPH 2. The assembled cupboard.

would, with tenoned rails, etc. There is, however, a much simpler way, which at this scale is quite acceptable, and with the door closed it is pretty nearly impossible to tell the difference. The first step of this method is to make the rails for the sides, top and bottom. Do not cut them to size at this stage, but leave them as one length for the moment. Put a rebate, deep enough to take the full thickness of the glass, right along one edge. Now measure very carefully the width of the opening for the door. Do not take it off the drawing, but measure it on the model. From this measurement subtract twice the thickness of the rail, not counting the rebate. For example, if the rail is $\frac{1}{4}''$ and the rebate $\frac{1}{8}''$ wide, twice the thickness of the rail, not counting the rebate, is $(\frac{1}{4}-\frac{1}{8})\times 2=\frac{1}{4}''$. These are not the actual dimensions for this model, as its rails are only $\frac{3}{16}''$ thick.

The next question is whether to use glass or one of the plastic substitutes. In this case I suggest a plastic substitute, which can usually be obtained in $\frac{1}{16}''$ thick sheets. It keeps the weight down, and with a door of this size hanging on miniature butts, weight could be important. Cut a piece of plastic to the size of the opening, less the thickness as worked out, making sure that it is nice and square. Cut the single-length rail into the appropriate size pieces and glue them in place to the edge of the plastic. One of the epoxy glues used sparingly works well. If you are making the Queen Anne-

PHOTOGRAPH 3. The completed door.

style cupboard, glue in the top shaped rails; if not, glue in the centre rails next. Note that the vertical one is continuous from top to bottom – see Photograph 3. Use a Decra Led strip (available from DIY shops) to make the leaded lights. The method is described on page 82, and the result is a very acceptable door, fairly simply made.

It now needs to be hung on a pair of butt hinges fitted outside. I long ago came to the conclusion that making butts is a bit of a waste of time, unless they are a special shape, in which case you might have to. Generally it is much better to purchase them, together with some fixing pins. I find that when fitting these small butts a piece of our old friend, double-sided tape – the thin sort, not the one used for carpet laying – is ideal, as it will hold the butt securely while the pins are inserted. Finally the knob has to be fitted. You can buy this as well, but it is easy enough to turn one for yourself. Provided that you have been reasonably careful putting the cupboard together, the door should be a good fit. If it is not, it should be easy enough to take a shaving from the wooden rails.

GUNS

There is no point in having a gun cupboard without the guns to go in it, and making a couple of 12-bores (Photograph 4), which really provides the finishing touch, is not difficult.

PHOTOGRAPH 4. A pair of 12-bores.

You will need a length of $\frac{1}{16}''$ brass tubing, a small piece of $\frac{1}{8}''$ square brass or, preferably, nickel silver, and some walnut to make the stocks. Follow Figure 4 when making the guns.

First, cut four lengths of brass tubing to make the barrels and solder them into pairs. Next, take a $\frac{1}{4}''$ length of the $\frac{1}{8}''$ metal and file a 'step' at either end, leaving about $\frac{1}{16}''$ in the centre. The 'step' needs to be equal to the depth of the barrels. Solder the barrels into the step at one end of the piece you have just made, making sure that they are all in line.

Brass barrels in 12-bore guns would look most peculiar, so it is necessary to blacken the barrels. You can, of course, just paint them, but somehow that does not look right. The answer is to blacken the brass chemically. A straightforward solution of one ounce of copper sulphate crystals dissolved in three ounces of water will work, although it will take some time and will blue rather than blacken them. To get it to work well you need to add a drop of silver nitrate solution. However, silver nitrate is very expensive, and if you can find a drop of used photographic fixer, the sort with which black and white photos are processed, it will work just as well. The brass barrels need to be absolutely grease-free before being put into the solution, and the degree of black you get is controlled by the length of time the brass is left to soak. When the guns are removed from the bath the black on the nickel silver parts should be gently filed or scraped away.

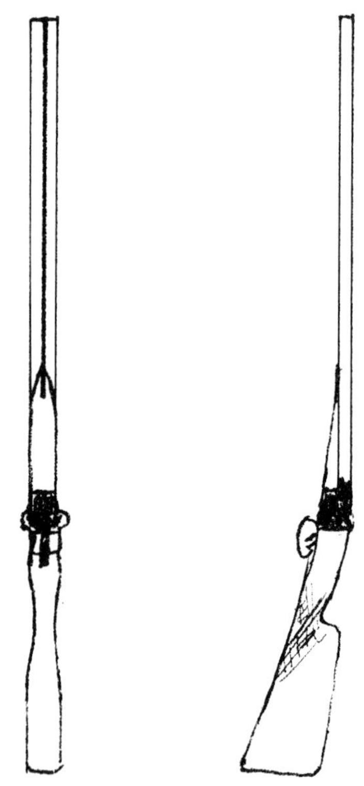

FIGURE 4. 12-bore shotgun.

While the barrels are drying, cut a piece of walnut to the shape of the stock and a smaller piece to make the forestock. With files and sandpaper, shape the stock and cut a step into the fore part to take the barrels. Glue the stock to the barrels, being careful to retain the correct angle. Glue the forestock to the underside of the barrels just forward of the nickel silver. A sliver of flattened brass tube forms the trigger guard just behind it. The final touch is to give all the wood parts a coat of varnish or your favourite finish.

If you haven't already done so, put in a shelf to support the tops of the gun barrels, and treat the entire cupboard with your selected finish.

PHOTOGRAPH 5. The finished corner gun cupboard ($4\frac{1}{2}''$ high × $2\frac{1}{2}''$ wide).

BUTTON-BACK WING CHAIR

ALTHOUGH these instructions are to make the button-back wing chair shown in the photographs, the drawings, with only minor alterations, can be used to make all kinds of variations of it. It could have thinner wings, different legs, even become a settee – the permutations are endless.

Similarly, the finishes are many. The chair pictured is finished in leather, and in Photograph 3 had just been treated with saddle soap, which gave this somewhat mottled appearance. Obviously, saddle soap was not the right finish for the leather used! But a quick trip to my supplier gave a suggestion for a possible solution. Three coats of dark leather stain, and three coats of dark tan shoe polish later and the end result (Photograph 4) is a big improvement. (This just goes to show that it is always worth trying to put things right before you give up, throw it away, and start again.) You can of course use all sorts of materials other than leather, while following the same method of upholstering.

CARCASS

This is one of those models which, quite honestly, could be made out of any sort of wood as long as it is smooth – even balsa if you have to! Just remember that the back legs are cut at the same time as the sides and are an integral part of them. Photograph 1 and Figure 1 show this. Following Figures 1, 2 and 3, mark out and cut the six pieces that form the carcass of the chair: two sides, back, seat and two front legs. The only

PHOTOGRAPH 1. The carcass of the wing chair ready for upholstery.

FIGURE 1. Front elevation.

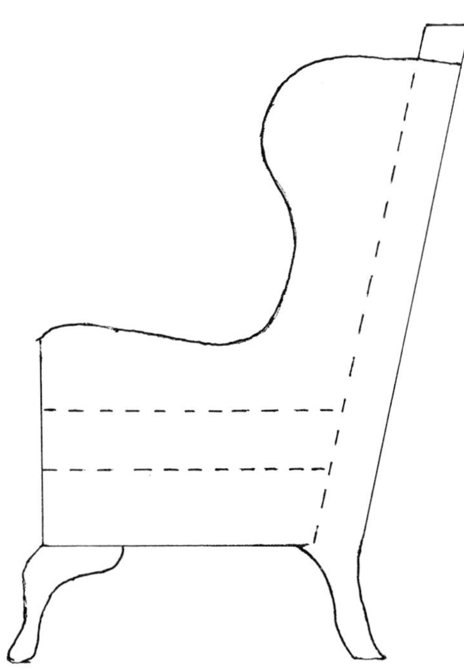

FIGURE 2. Side elevation.

FIGURE 3. Plan.

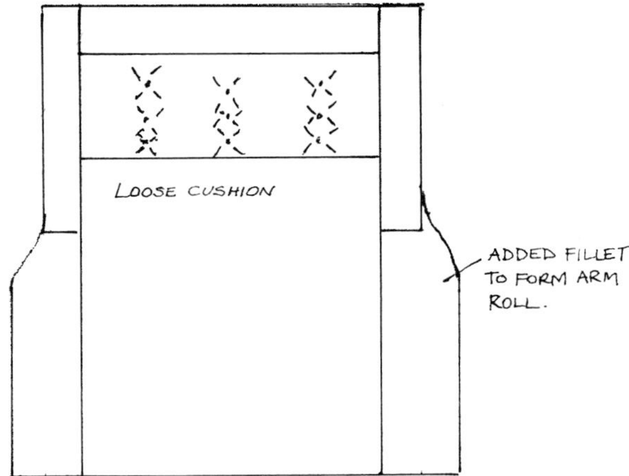

ones that are at all tricky are the front legs – mark them from the side elevation (Figure 2) and cut and shape them. (When you come to fix these front feet, glue them pointing very slightly outwards.) Glue the four main pieces together, leaving the front feet off for the time being. What could be simpler? You have now completed the framework of the chair.

Cut in half, lengthwise, a short piece of ½″ dowel. Glue a half to the outside of each of the chair sides to form the arm swells. Sand the back end of this dowel into a smooth curve that disappears just where the wing starts to swell out.

UPHOLSTERY

When deciding what to cover your first attempted chair with, pick a material without a large pattern repeat, as that makes it easier to lose the joins. If you are handy with a needle you may care to sew a semi-loose cover for the framework. If, like me, you aren't, then Copydex is the answer.

First, cut a paper templet to the shape of the inside of the sides (see Figure 2), then cut out the material and glue it in place. If you are using a thin material, then by all means turn it over the edge of the wings, but make sure that it is nicked so as not to get too many thicknesses on the arms.

Next, cut a piece to cover the arm swells from the top to just under the finish of the dowel. Alternatively, you can stick the arms the other way, with the material running along the arms and down the front of them – it just depends which is the best way for the pattern you have chosen. Remember – there are no hard and fast rules. If it *looks* right, it *is* right.

FIGURE 4. Section A–A.

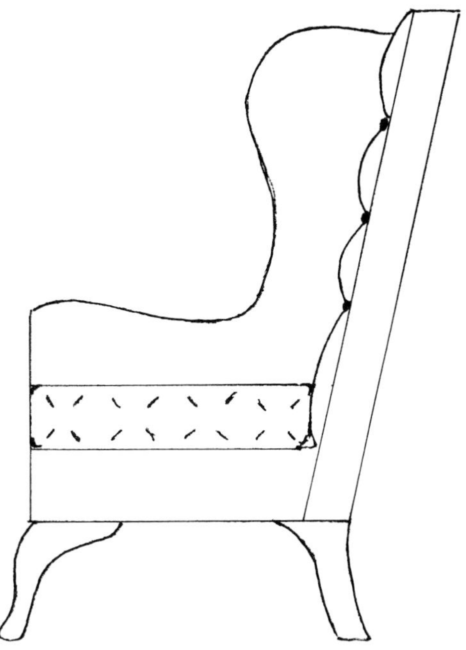

Now cover the outside of the wings. The object is to make sure the join is between the side and the arm, just below the bulge of the arm, so that it is largely hidden. The back of the chair can be covered with one piece. This leaves two strips on either wing above the arm rest, a small strip along the top of the back, and a strip along the front below the seat cushion.

BUTTONING

The next job is to make the back cushion and the seat. For the back, cut a piece of card the same width as between the wings and mark on it the positions of the buttons in your chosen pattern. Remember to allow extra space around the card if you are using a thick covering like leather, or you will find that when finished the cushion is too bulky. Take a piece of foam sheet about $\frac{1}{2}''$ thick and cut a piece slightly smaller than the card. Drill the card where you have marked it, and putting the foam between the covering and the card, sew through both the foam and covering, and back again. It does not matter if you go through the same hole in the card, but move the hole slightly in the covering, or when you attempt to pull the thread to make the button effect, it will pull straight through – no button! Go straight to the next hole without cutting the thread, but after each hole make a half-hitch and carry on until all the marks are done – Photograph 2 illustrates this stage. It sounds a lot more complicated than it is, and once you get the hang of it you will wonder why it ever sounded difficult.

Turn the back so that the buttoned surface is pointing

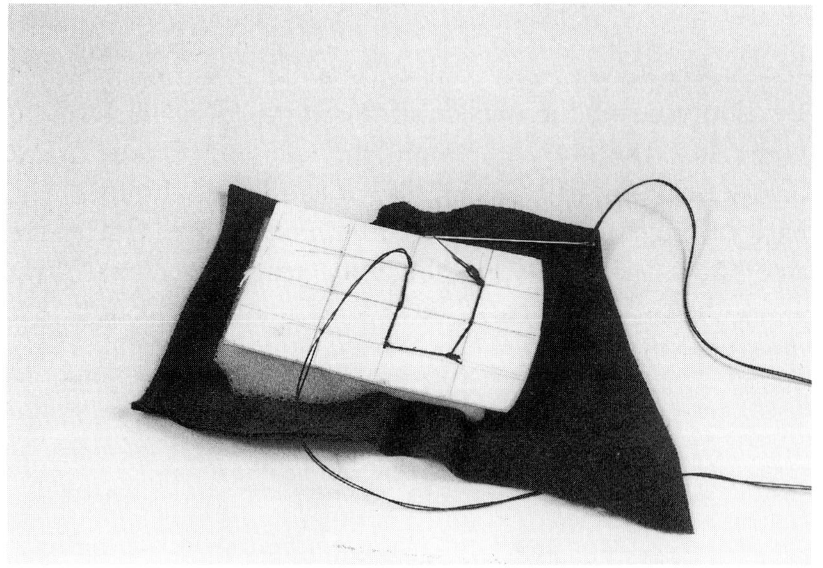

PHOTOGRAPH 2. Forming the button back.

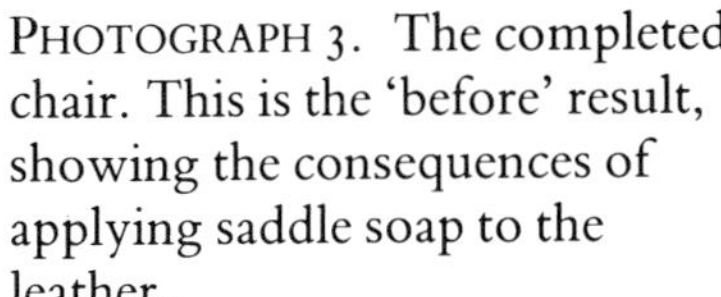

PHOTOGRAPH 3. The completed chair. This is the 'before' result, showing the consequences of applying saddle soap to the leather.

PHOTOGRAPH 4. The transformed upholstery, after treatment with dark leather stain and dark tan shoe polish.

downwards and gently pull two opposite sides over the back of the card and glue in place. Now do the same with the other two sides. If you are using thin material you will probably get away with folding the corners, but if the material is thicker you may need to cut and trim them. When the glue has dried, place the cushion between the wings and glue it to the back. The seat can be made in the same way, but if you have ever sat on a buttoned chair seat for any length of time you will know that you would not inflict the experience even on a doll. You can still make the seat in the same way as the back, but leave out the buttoning bit. Again, glue it into place.

This just leaves the front legs to be glued on, and finished with a little stain. There you have an upholstered chair fit for any setting.

SNOOKER TABLE AND ACCESSORIES

THIS is the one project for which the drawings are not full-size in inch to the foot scale. The reason for this is that a full-size snooker table is 12 feet long and 6 feet wide, which means 1 foot by 6 inches in our scale! But for once this is not all that important, as it is really just a large table with all the important bits happening at the corners and in the middle. You can of course build a smaller table, but please look up the dimensions first as a half-size table is not 6 feet by 3 feet. The drawings, description and photographs are all for a full-size table.

TABLE TOP

The table top is designed to be made from easily obtainable materials. To begin with, the basic table is made from a 12″ section of 6″ wide mahogany-covered chipboard shelving, $\frac{1}{2}$″ thick. This is already edged on the two long sides, and only needs iron-on edging on the two short sides. Pick the best face, sand it smooth, and apply a covering of Fablon green baize finish. This is self-adhesive, but it is a good idea to leave the top under a weight, if possible for at least a couple of days. You now need to cut the holes for the pockets at the four corners and the middle of both sides. These pockets full size are $3\frac{1}{2}$″ in diameter, i.e. $\frac{5}{16}$″ in the model, and need to be

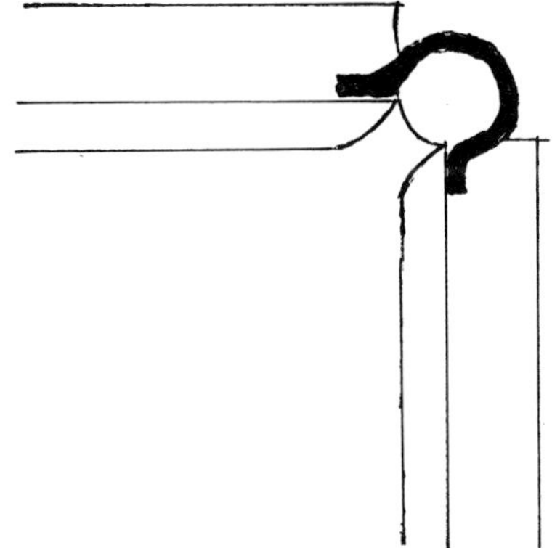

FIGURE 1a. Detail at corners.

FIGURE 1b. Detail at centre pocket.

cut to half their diameter into the table so that they form semicircular indents. See Figures 1a and 1b.

LEGS

To make the eight legs, obtain some ½″ mahogany-type dowel and turn up the legs to the profiles shown in Figure 2.

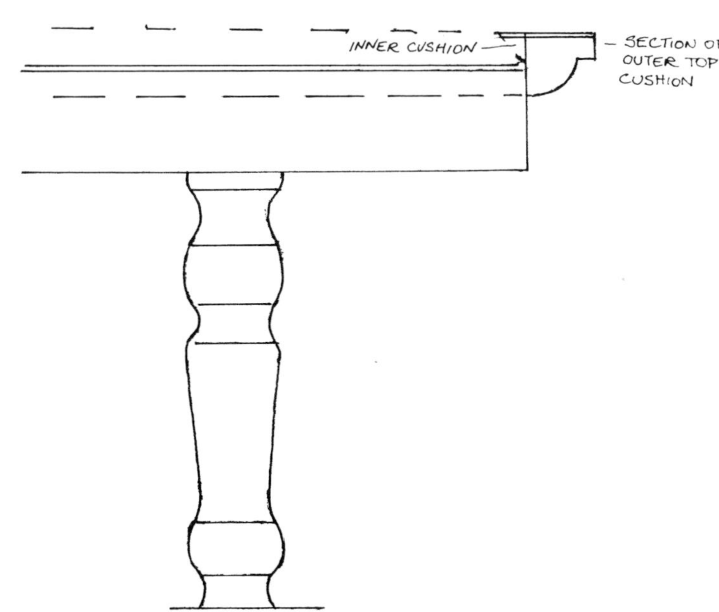

FIGURE 2. Detail of legs and cushions.

The reason I suggest using $\frac{1}{2}''$ dowel is because it is then possible to turn the legs using a drill, files and sandpaper, so that the whole project can be made without the use of a lathe. Seal and polish the legs before fixing them to the table. Use a piece of dowel to fix one at each corner just inside the pocket. Make sure that the maximum diameter is level with the long edge of the table. The remaining four legs go two each side, spaced equidistantly along the long edge. If you have cut all the legs accurately, and fixed them squarely, the table should stand solidly on all eight legs.

CUSHIONS

When you are buying the dowel, look at the same time for a section similar to that shown in Figure 2 and which can be seen in Photograph 1. Most of the large DIY stores carry both. It does not have to be exactly the same, just similar. This will form the outer part of the top cushion, and should be cut into lengths to fit between the pockets. It is quite in order to have square ends to these sections. The pieces need to be glued to the table so that they are $\frac{1}{8}''$ above the surface of the baize. The easiest way to achieve this is to pack the table

PHOTOGRAPH 1. Corner pocket showing outer part of cushion.

top so that it is fixed, upside down, $\frac{1}{8}''$ above a flat surface. It is then possible to work your way round, gluing each section to the table, certain that each will be the required height above the table top.

The next thing to make is the inner part of the top cushions. This is a little more fiddly as in the full-size table they only project over the table top by not more than 2″ and not less than $1\frac{1}{2}''$. This means you need to produce a triangular-section piece of timber $\frac{1}{8}''$ by $\frac{1}{8}''$ covered with green Fablon. This time it is not enough to trust to the self-adhesive properties of the Fablon – it will need reinforcing with a good adhesive. This is another of those occasions when our old friend the masking tape comes into its own. Cut the triangular-section wood into lengths corresponding to the spaces between the pockets. Lay a length of masking tape, sticky side up, on the bench and lay the strip of Fablon on it. Spread the glue on the Fablon, put the wood in the centre, and turn the masking tape edge to edge. By pressing along the tape with your fingers, it is possible to get the wood into really close contact with the Fablon. It can remain in the tape until you feel sure that it has got a good hold. Remember, there is little air to aid drying, so you must allow a little longer than usual for this. In fact it is probably as well to use a chemical reaction glue such as Araldite. When dry, peel the masking tape from the cushion. The ends should be chamfered to form a smooth entry to the pockets. Before fixing these pieces it is a good idea to polish, or finish as you wish, the outer top rails. This will save you spoiling the Fablon. The newly formed cushions can be glued to the outer wooden ones in such a way that the tops of both are level with each other. It is easier to touch in the chamfered ends with paint rather than attempt to attach Fablon to them.

POCKET FRAMEWORK

Now is the time to indulge in a little metalwork, firstly making the framework for the pockets. Trying to bend $\frac{1}{16}''$ metal strip on the flat is very difficult. I suggest that you use $\frac{1}{16}''$ diameter brass tube, initially bent around a $\frac{5}{16}''$ drill shank, and then to the shapes shown in Figures 1a and 1b. When you are happy with the shape, take a hammer and flatten the tube – gently, or you will have hammer marks all over the brass. These should then be let into the timber tops on either side of the pockets to form the top rail.

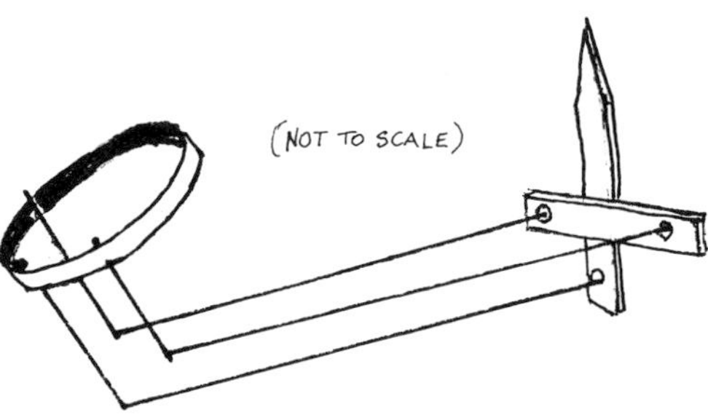

FIGURE 3. Pocket runner assembly.

The second part of the metalwork consists of forming the runners which collect and hold the balls when potted – see Figure 3. The first part of this job is to make up a small cross and drill three $\frac{1}{16}''$ holes in the centre and cross arms. Using this as a templet, drill the same diameter holes in a scrap piece of wood. Cut three pieces of $\frac{1}{16}''$ diameter brass

PHOTOGRAPH 2. Centre pocket.

wire – slightly longer than required, to allow for setting up in the pre-drilled holes in the wood. Thread them through the holes in the cross, set them up in the wood and solder them firmly into position. You will now have a cross with three long pieces of wire at right angles. Remove and clean up the short wires that went into the wood. Measuring the required distance along the wires from the cross, bend the ends to an angle of around 75°F. From a length of $\frac{11}{32}''$ outside-diameter brass tube (sorry, but that is what it measures; all the brass can be obtained from a K & S Metal Center, which can be found in most good model shops), slice off a number of $\frac{1}{16}''$ rings and solder the three wires to the insides of these rings. Make sure that the balls cannot drop out between the wires! (This is much easier than it sounds.)

FRENCH KNITTING

To complete the pockets you need to make the string piece which joins together the top rail and the runner. Those of you who are old enough may remember something you did at school called French knitting. It involved old wool, and a

PHOTOGRAPH 3. 'Knitting' the pockets.

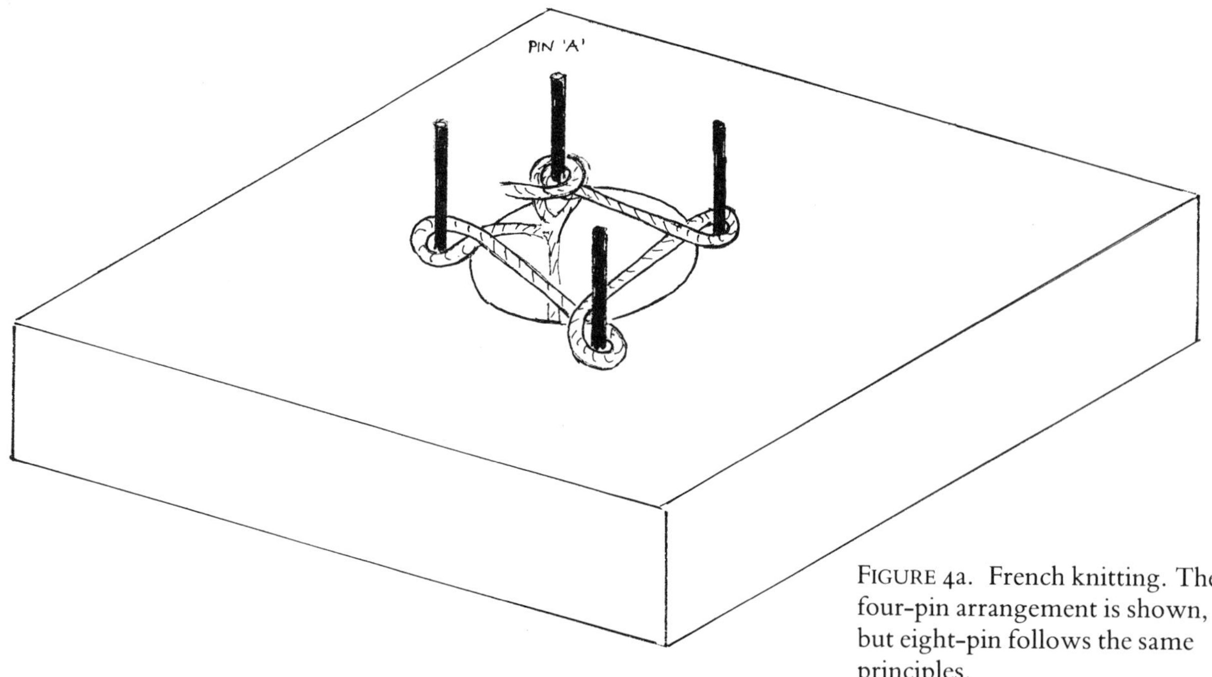

FIGURE 4a. French knitting. The four-pin arrangement is shown, but eight-pin follows the same principles.

cotton reel with four pins in the top. For those of you who have forgotten or have never even heard of it, this form of knitting consists of making a half-hitch round each pin in turn, then lifting the bottom turn over the pin, always retaining just one turn on each pin, and pulling the resulting tube through the middle of the cotton reel. Four pins and a cotton reel used to be standard, but to make pockets for the snooker table you need a bigger hole and eight pins. Drill a $\frac{3}{8}''$ hole in a $\frac{1}{2}''$ piece of wood, sand the edges of the hole so as not to snag the thread, and put eight veneer pins equidistantly round the hole and about $\frac{1}{4}''$ away from it. Make six short lengths of tube using a fine crochet thread, trying to work it loosely. It can get very tight and you may find yourself fighting it. You will also find that it helps to use a darning needle to lift the lower turn up and over. Figures 4a, b and c should make the method clear. Finally, glue the knitted tubes to the rings on the runners, the brass rail on the table, and the table side of the pocket hole. A small hole will enable the pointed end of the cross to be pushed up into the top rail of the table to hold the other end of the runner. When the glue has dried, cut off the excess above the brass rail and table.

That completes the table and leaves only the accessories.

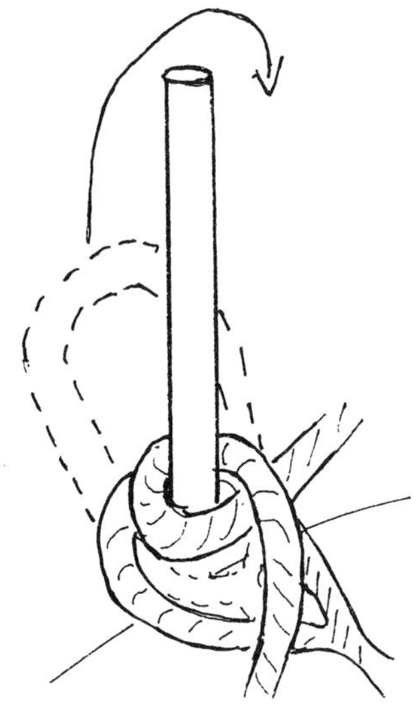

FIGURE 4b. Pin 'A' showing the movement of the loop.

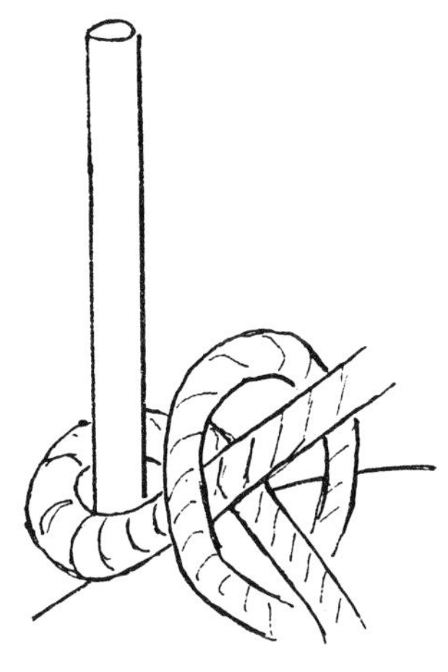

FIGURE 4c. Pin 'A' showing the completion of the stitch. Repeat this as required.

ACCESSORIES

BALLS Let us start with the balls, which are 22 in number: 15 red, and one each white, yellow, green, brown, blue, pink, and black. When I was making the prototype for this model, a considerable amount of time was spent experimenting with the best way to make the balls. I tried every thing, from turning them out of plastic knitting needles to moulding them out of Fimo – without much success. In the end, I arrived at the method I now suggest as being the easiest and producing a reasonable result. The trouble is that snooker balls are only $2\frac{1}{16}''$ in diameter, which is about $\frac{5}{64}''$ at scale, and the nearest obtainable thing to that is 4mm ball bearings. If you look in the Yellow Pages for a bearing supplier, they will be able to help you. You may have to buy a hundred, but when your friends see your superb set of miniature snooker balls you will know that it was all worth it.

The secret of painting them is to use ordinary Humbrol enamel model paint. On a spare piece of wood, place a strip of double-sided tape, and lay the 22 balls on it, having first degreased them in meths or a similar spirit. Paint the top half of each ball (the stickiness of the tape will stop them rolling about). Leave them overnight, or until they dry, and roll each ball over. Now paint the exposed, unpainted half. In this way you avoid creating ridges of paint and the balls will still roll smoothly.

TRIANGLE This is made from mahogany strips $14'' \times 2'' \times \frac{3}{4}''$ full size, mitred at the corners, You may need to adjust the size to make sure it will take all the 15 red balls.

CUES Full-size cues must be at least 3 feet long, and are normally about 4′10″. At the butt end they are only just over 1″ in diameter, which makes turning them almost impossible. By far the easiest way is to start with a dowel, if you can find one, or a prepared strip, and scrape and sandpaper. There are two other types of cue, known as rests. There is the rest in the form of a cross, made from either plastic or

PHOTOGRAPH 4. The snooker table and accessories.

metal, and the 'spider', which provides a bridge of extra height. Both of these come in two lengths, the 'half-butt' (8 feet long), and the 'long rest' (12 feet long). if you wish to make a full set, that means two cross-shaped rests and two 'spiders', together with the appropriate cues to match. Not at all difficult, but rather time-consuming.

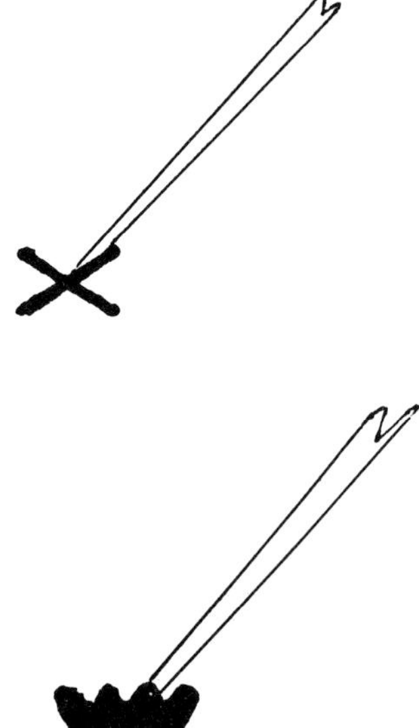

FIGURE 5. The spider and rest.

SCOREBOARD This is made from a piece of mahogany, lipped and marked out as in Figure 5. The markers above and below the figures run on metal runners, and the top one is usually marked with a spot. The best way to represent this is with a length of 00 gauge model railway track let into the mahogany, with a small piece of filed brass rod to run along it. Numbers can be Letraset, or hand-painted if you have a very steady hand.

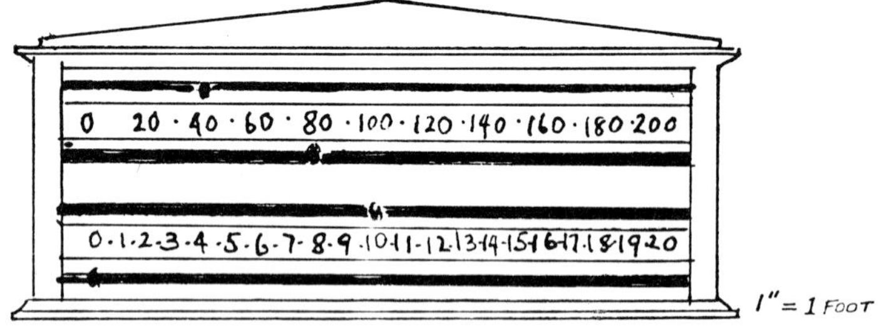

FIGURE 6. The scoreboard.

Figure 7 shows the table with lines marked on, and Photograph 4 the complete model accessories. You are going to need a large dolls' house to fit a full-size table in, but it could form the basis of a lovely room setting.

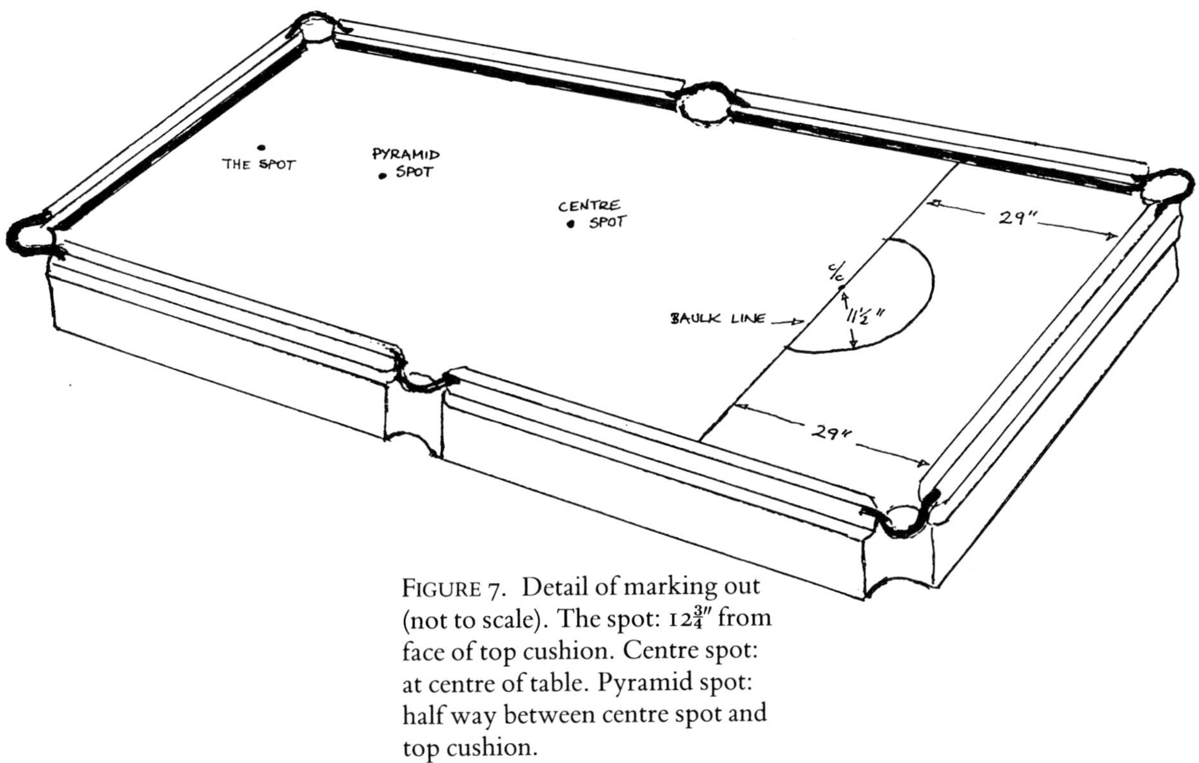

FIGURE 7. Detail of marking out (not to scale). The spot: 12¾" from face of top cushion. Centre spot: at centre of table. Pyramid spot: half way between centre spot and top cushion.

ADAM-STYLE FIREPLACE

ALTHOUGH this is one of the simpler projects, it is by no means the least spectacular. It creates an excellent effect, whether in a dolls' house or a room setting.

TIMBER

Most Adam fireplaces are made of one of the pines, but for a model, pine has too coarse a grain and thus does not look right. It is better to use something like ramin, which has the same straw colour and a grain which is more in proportion. This applies even if you intend to paint the finished fireplace.

MAIN PARTS

Having chosen and prepared your timber to the correct size, start by laying out the main parts. It is easiest to lay them on double-sided tape on a spare piece of ply or hardboard. As Photograph 1 shows, there are only five main parts: the two sides, the mantel and its blocked-out centre, and the over-shelf. All the sizes can be taken from Figure 1. The only tricky part of this, and in fact of the whole operation, is to cut the dished recesses in the mantel. The easy way to do this is to use a small ball-shaped cutter and a pillar drill with a fine feed, coupled with a method of controlling the movement of the workpiece – the ideal tool for which is the Emco-Unimat 3. However, it is hardly worth the cost of a Unimat just for this job, and there are several other ways it can be done. One

PHOTOGRAPH 1. The basic parts.

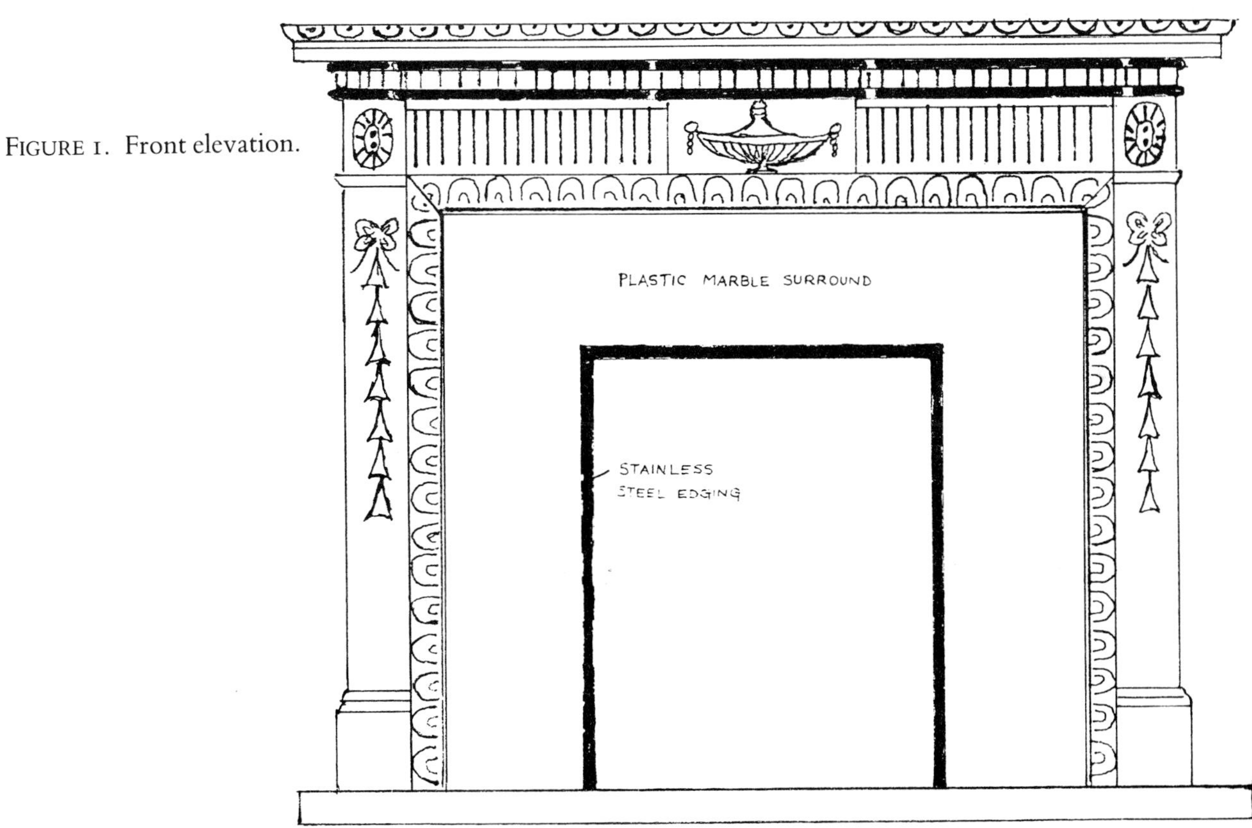

FIGURE 1. Front elevation.

method I followed, in the days before I owned any machine tools, was to make up a piece of steel to the shape of the rebate, heat it in a gas flame, and burn each one – slow but effective. A soldering iron would probably work just as well. Another method could be to cut each one individually with a small gouge. This is by no means an exhaustive list, but whatever method you elect, after cutting the mantel, assemble the fireplace from the five pieces on the board. This is the basic fireplace, and all the rest is decoration, which will be chosen to suit yourself.

MOULDINGS

There are several firms who are able to supply Adam-style mouldings suitable for use on this type of fireplace, and unless you have either some pretty sophisticated machinery or endless patience, it is easier to buy these mouldings. They do not always have to come from a model supplier – the local DIY shop can often be a source of inspiration at reasonable cost. Figure 2 shows an example of the kind of results which can be achieved. Do not always feel obliged to use the whole moulding as supplied, but be prepared to look at it from different angles and cut the portion you require.

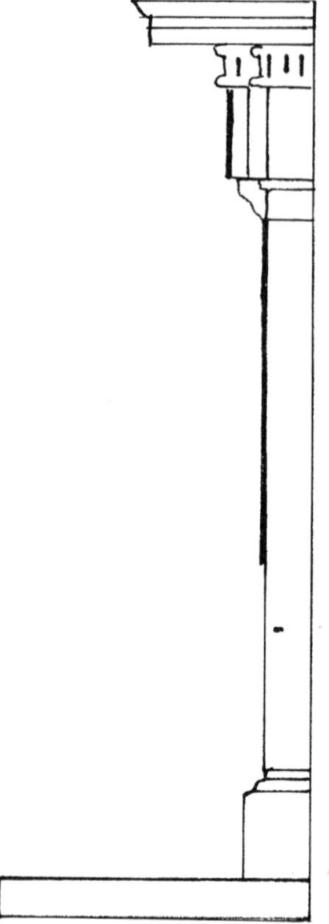

FIGURE 2. Side elevation.

Having selected your mouldings, the rest is a matter of cutting mitres, for which all you need is a small homemade bench saddle (see the chapter on Tools and Tips) with mitre cuts in the stop, a razor saw, a little glue, and a whole lot of patience.

CARVED RELIEFS

The last part of the decoration is the five carved reliefs (Figure 3) which need to be marked out and cut away, then stuck on. Choose your wood carefully for these. If, like me, carving is not your strong suit, a softwood like basswood or, for once, balsa, has a lot to recommend it, as the detail will be blurred by the nature of the wood. If, on the other hand, you are quite good at carving, then use a hardwood like holly or box, where all the detail will stand out to be admired and the fireplace will look all the better for it.

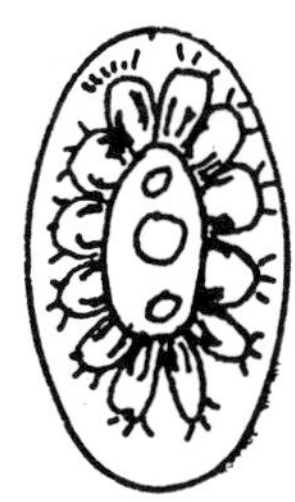

FIGURE 3. Detail of carvings (not to scale).

INFILL

Now is the time to think about the infill surrounding the actual fire – in this case it is marble to match the hearth. You can of course use real marble, and when chosen with care there is nothing to compare with it, even in miniature. It is, however, expensive and not easy to work with, and if you can find a mason to cut and prepare it for you – well – lucky you! The fireplace in the photograph has marble of much humbler origins, in fact it is a plastic tile, as sold in DIY shops. Having said this, there is little else to add. Cut the plastic to shape and insert it between the side pieces. It helps to fit the infill before the last pieces of moulding, as they will form a rebate and allow the whole fireplace to sit back against the wall. The plastic tile comes complete with a polystyrene backing, which makes it exactly the right height for the hearth upon which the fireplace happily sits.

FINISHING

Finishing is a matter of choice, and will be dictated by the decor of the room. The example described here is finished in a natural polish with a stainless surround to the fire opening. The fire itself can be as elaborate as one cares to make it –

from a piece of black paper with a bowl of flowers in front, to the full works of flickering flames, fire dogs, etc. Again, it will depend on the room setting.

PHOTOGRAPH 2. The finished fireplace.

GEORGIAN DRUM TABLE

THIS table (*circa* 1760), from the great age of English furniture, is more complicated, but really no more difficult, than the Refectory Table (see page 12). It will just take a bit longer and maybe make you scratch your head now and again. This is one of those pieces where a lathe, while not absolutely essential, will make things a lot easier. The full-size table has two ordinary drawers, two swivel drawers and four dummy drawers. It is made from mahogany, and there is no reason not to use the same timber for the miniature. You will also need some $\frac{1}{16}''$ plywood, a small piece of $\frac{1}{4}''$ plywood, some leather, and mahogany veneer. Figure 1 shows all the elements of the top of the table before you begin.

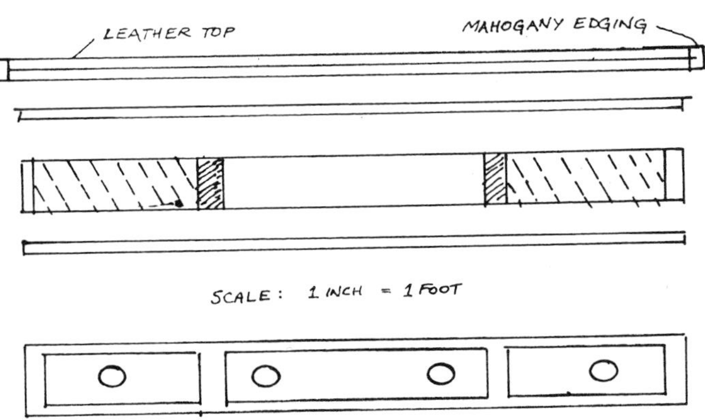

FIGURE 1. The elements of the table top.

CARCASS

The first job is to make the carcassing of the table. To start with, cut three circles of $\frac{1}{16}''$ plywood, and one of $\frac{1}{4}''$. If you have the use of a lathe, centre drill, thread a bolt through, and true them all up to a diameter of $3\frac{3}{8}''$. No lathe? Not to worry. Hold the discs together with small pieces of double-sided tape, and clean them up with file and sandpaper. It will take a little longer, but the end result will be just as good. Next, prepare some $\frac{1}{4}''$ thick timber to make up the shapes described as **A** and **B** in Figures 2a and 2b. Having carefully marked out one of your $\frac{1}{16}''$ circles, cut and fit all the carcassing pieces as shown in Figures 2a and 2b. Please note that the pieces marked **A** in Figure 2a are solid. The only other thing to be careful about is to get the distances exactly right when setting out, as there is a dummy drawer between each real one.

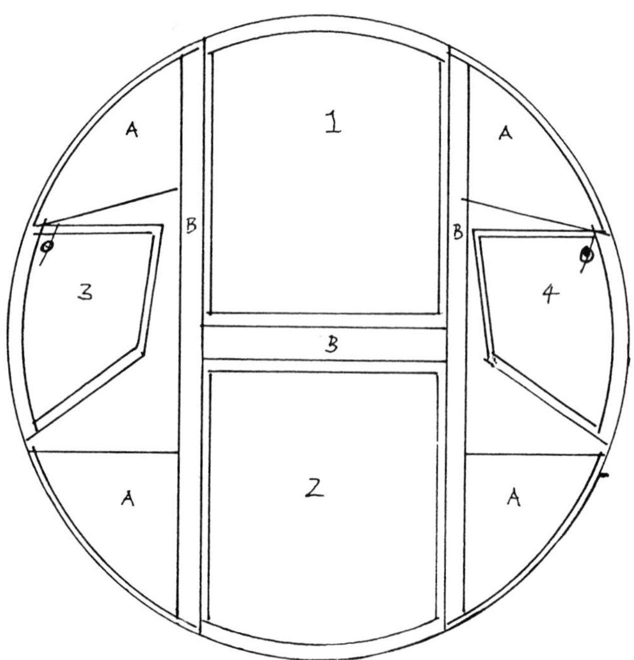

FIGURE 2a. Plan, with top $\frac{1}{16}''$ ply removed.

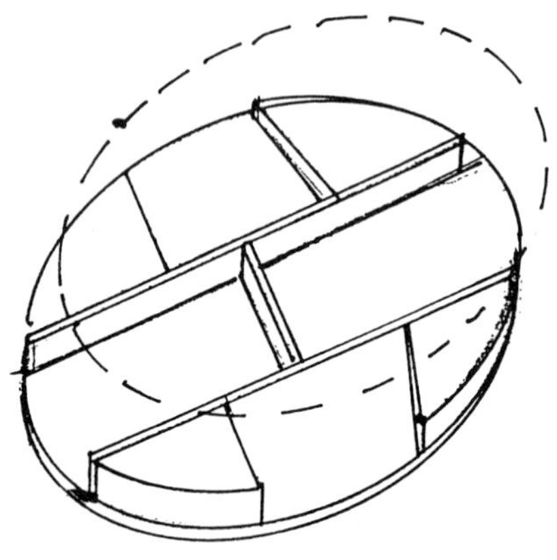

FIGURE 2b. Diagrammatic view of table top carcassing.

DRAWERS

It is easier to make the four drawers next, before adding the top piece of $\frac{1}{16}''$ plywood. Each drawer consists of five pieces, of which the front is the most important. There is the fancy way of making them, or if you do not feel up to that, there is a much simpler way. It goes like this: cut a piece of $\frac{1}{16}''$ plywood to the shape of the bottom of the drawer and to it glue the curved front of the drawer. Remember to reduce the height of the front so that the overall height of the drawer, including the base, is no more than $\frac{1}{4}''$, and to reduce the width of the front by the thickness of the two sides (see Figure 3). Then glue on the two sides, and finally the back. The sides and back can also be made from $\frac{1}{16}''$ plywood. As the drawer will eventually be veneered, the end result will be perfectly acceptable.

PHOTOGRAPH 1. The carcass of the table top and drawers.

The other way to build the drawer is almost as you would for full size. This will take you twice as long, and probably cause a blue halo to encircle the working area at times, but think of the pleasure you will get when you point out to admiring onlookers the dovetails on the drawer fronts!

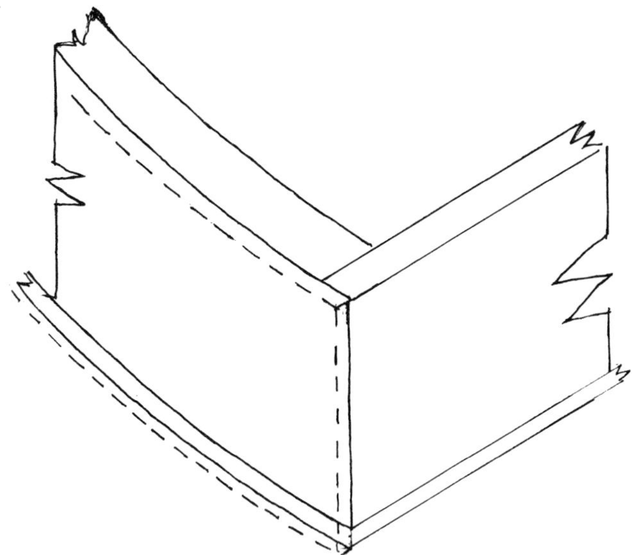

FIGURE 3. Detail of simple drawer front. The dotted line shows the veneer front.

To do it this way more tools will make things much easier – well, one really – a miniature drill, a cutter of one sort or another to rebate the bottom of the drawer, and a dentists' drill to form the dovetails. Dentists use a drill called an 'inverted cone', which looks exactly as the name implies, and is the perfect shape for dovetails. The drills come in six sizes, so from the full range it is possible to pick just the right one for the size of drawer. Next time you have to visit your dentist, see if you can persuade him to let you have his blunt – for teeth, that is – cutters, they really are worth their weight in gold to miniaturists.

So back to the drawers. Again, start with a plywood bottom (Figure 2a, areas 1 and 2), but cut the drawer front to the full depth and width. On the bottom of the front, cut a rebate deep enough for the plywood bottom, and about half the width of the front. Shape the drawer bottom to fit and glue up. If you are prepared to attempt dovetailing the drawer sides, see Figure 4, you either know how to mark out and cut a dovetail, or you are prepared to look it up.

Just two little tips: there is no need to make as many joints as you would in a full-size drawer, and when cutting the dovetails on the sides, use a scrap piece of wood to back up the side and cut right through into the scrap – it will stop the dovetails breaking off.

Make up all four drawers at the same time and fit them into the carcassed bottom half of the table. Remember, drawers **1** and **2** are the normal pull-out type of drawer, while **3** and **4** are swivel drawers, hence the strange shape.

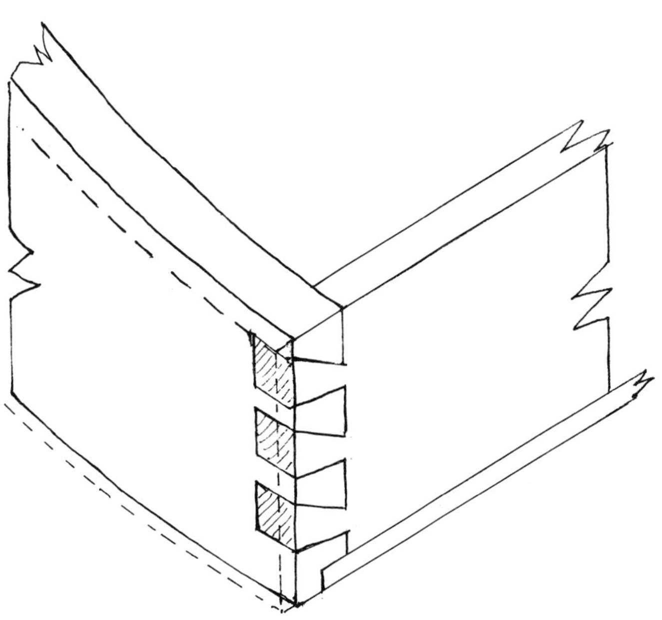

FIGURE 4. Detail of dovetail corner on the more difficult drawer front.

VENEERING

With all the drawers made, it is time to glue the second $\frac{1}{16}''$ plywood disc to the first, on top of the carcassing, and clean it up all round. Make sure that all the drawers fit snugly and will open easily. Clearly mark on the newly fixed disc the extent of the drawer openings. Next, you need to veneer the edge of the table top and all the drawer fronts. The greatest asset when doing this part of the job is a roll of $\frac{3}{4}''$ masking tape, as it can be made to act as all kinds of spare hands, and for this particular job it would be useful to be equipped like an octopus.

Remove the drawers. Cut a strip of veneer about $\frac{1}{2}''$ wide and long enough to encircle the table. It should bend around this diameter cold, but if in any doubt, hold it in the steam from a boiling kettle just to soften it. Mark it and cut either a butt joint or a scarf joint. Apply the glue and wrap the veneer round, securing it tightly with the aid of the masking tape. Now you can see what I mean about the octopus! It will also be useful later on if you make sure that there is a layer of tape all round. Put it aside to dry and veneer the drawer fronts, again using masking tape.

Now that you are thoroughly familiar with the technique of veneering, you might as well do some more, this time on the $\frac{1}{4}''$ plywood disc that was cut right at the beginning. This time you need two layers of veneer, and the first layer must *not* stick to the plywood, as the idea is to use it to form a ring of veneer which will become the mahogany rim edging of the table top. The easiest way is to use a small piece of double-sided tape at the joint of the first layer of veneer, which will hold it in place while you apply the second layer. Make the centre of the second layer cover the joint on the first and bind it all up securely with masking tape. Set it aside to dry and take a well-earned rest!

When it is dry, without removing the masking tape, cut and trim the veneer level with both sides of the top. If you use a very sharp blade and take shallow cuts, finishing with a file, you will find that it is possible to do this without splitting any of the veneer away. It is worth taking lots of time over this, because if you do split off the veneer, you may have to start all over again.

Having made both sides level, it remains to remove the veneer from the openings for the drawers. You should have these clearly marked, and it is a matter of small cuts, lots of patience and softly, softly. Now you can remove the masking tape, *gently*! With a bit of luck you should now have a nicely veneered top for your table. Do the same thing for the drawers. Mark in the dummy drawers with a black biro, preferably a fine one. Sand, seal and apply your choice of finish. Put the top to one side while you make the drawer pulls.

DRAWER PULLS

For the drawer pulls you will need: a length of $\frac{1}{8}''$ brass rod, a sheet of 0.005 brass, and some 0.025 wire (mine is all ex-transformer wiring – every time an old wireless, or anything with coils in it, comes to hand, into the box it goes. Over the years it has become quite a collection, and can usually provide a suitable wire.)

PHOTOGRAPH 2. Parts for making the drawer pulls.

Take the brass rod and wrap about $\frac{1}{2}''$ of tight turns of the wire around it, see Photograph 2. Using a razor saw, cut through the wire along the length of the rod – this will give you a number of individual rings. Separate them, squeeze the ends together and apply a dab of superglue. You will now have number of rings of copper wire. Find some much finer wire, a separated wire from a piece of flex is ideal. Cut off about an inch, thread it through a ring, twist it tight and cut off, leaving about a $\frac{1}{4}''$ for fixing.

Lastly you will need some $\frac{1}{8}''$ brass discs which are punched from the 0.005 sheet using the squared end of a piece of rod. You might get away with a piece of the brass one, but a mild steel piece would be better, or hardened steel better still. To get nice clean punchings, lay the brass sheet on an old piece of lead and punch into that.

Drill the drawer fronts where necessary and secure the rings with a touch of glue. The brass punchings are glued under the rings for the finishing touch. There are two pulls on the big drawers and one to each of the others, including the dummies.

COMPLETING THE TOP

Take the third $\frac{1}{16}''$ plywood disc and to it glue the leather top. Ordinary white woodworking glue is perfect, and you will find that leather can be worked on the reverse side with sandpaper if it is too thick. Trim the surplus leather when the glue is really dry. Now take the $\frac{1}{4}''$ disc enclosed by the two layers of veneer, which should still have the masking tape around it, and trim one face only. Release the ring of veneer from the plywood and finish the trimmed face – you do not want to have to sand it after it is fixed. Lay the top, leather side down, on a smooth, flat surface. Try the ring. It should just slip over and be a nice tight fit, but the chances are that it won't! Too tight is easy – sand the edge of the top. Too slack? Probably the easiest way to put this right is to make a sawcut in the ring and a new butt joint. When the fit is right and the glue has dried, clean up the untrimmed side of the ring, and there you have your leather-covered top with a mahogany edging.

The leather top of the real table is tooled, and this is shown in Figure 5, but I am not sure that it is really worth all the effort involved. If you want to do it, I suggest you consult either an article or book on bookbinding and follow the same basic procedures. The whole process of fitting a leather-topped table top increases the amount of work

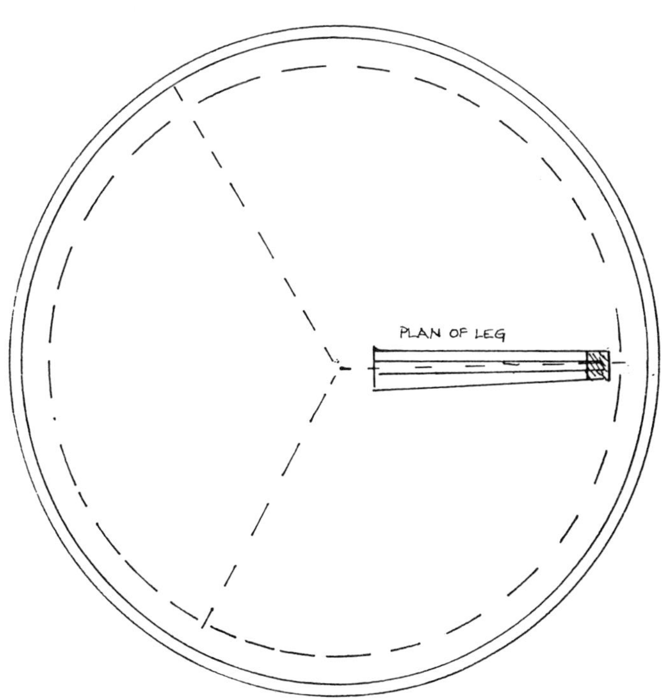

FIGURE 5. Plan, showing tooled pattern on leather top and positions of legs underneath.

involved in making the piece, and if you wish to simplify the whole thing, just fit a polished mahogany disc.

TRIPOD LEG

The final part of the job is to make up and fit the tripod leg.

Chuck a piece of ½″ square mahogany, and turn the centre pedestal to the shape and size shown in Figure 6, leaving a small peg on the top for locating purposes. Cut three legs to the shape and thickness shown (also Figure 5) and, holding them together with double-sided tape, do the final cleaning and sanding all together. On the end of each leg is a brass casing to which the castor is fitted, see Figure 7. Make the casings from ⅛″ square brass tube, which most good model shops should stock. (Most of the better shops do now keep short lengths of brass in all sorts of profiles.) Cut off pieces about ⅛″ long and solder a flat plate to one end of each. Clean them up with a file and you should have three

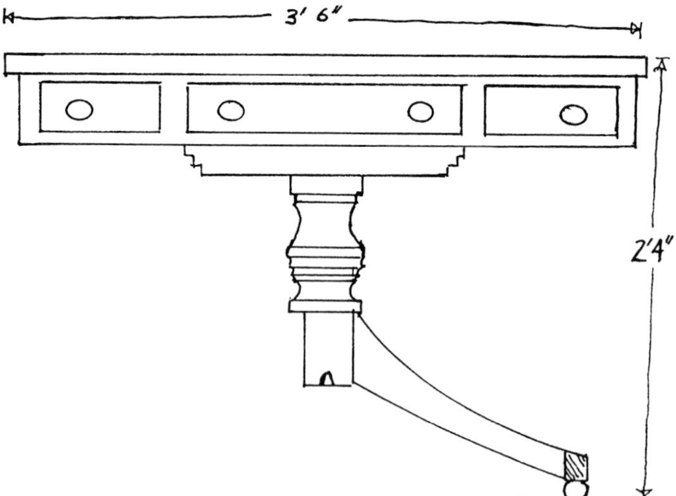

FIGURE 6. Elevation.

brass caps to fit the legs. Cut the legs to fit into the brass ends, and fix with a spot of glue.

I do not think it is worth all the effort of trying to make moving castors. Of course it is possible, but I feel that it comes more into the category of watchmaking, and I must admit to never having managed to make castors that were satisfactory (although I suspect the way to do it probably lies in etching). To make a reasonable replica, use the $\frac{1}{8}$″ brass

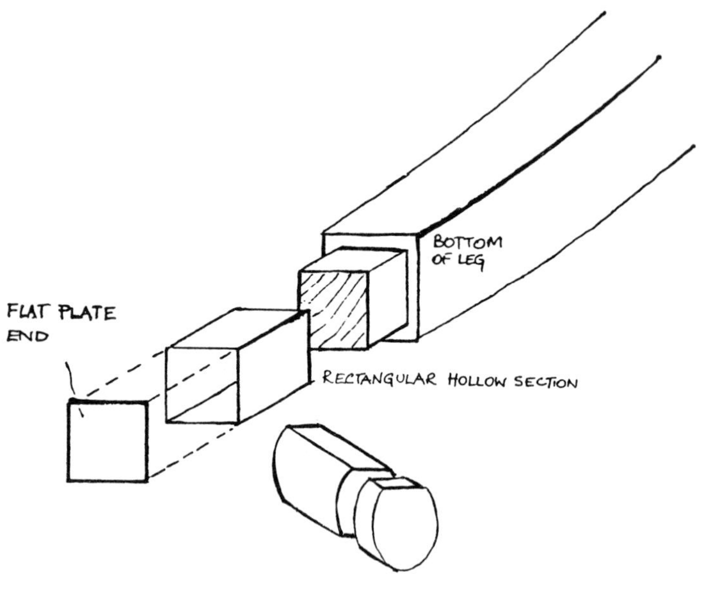

FIGURE 7. Exploded detail of brass leg ends and castors.

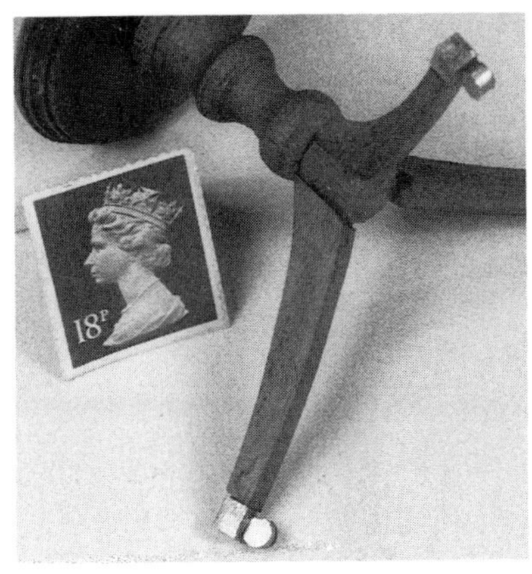

PHOTOGRAPH 3. The tripod leg in detail.

rod, file a flat on a short length and cut off three pieces about $\frac{1}{16}''$ wide. Fix them to the undersides of the brass-cased leg ends with a touch of superglue. Photograph 3 shows the finished legs.

ASSEMBLY

The final assembly can now take place. To find the correct intervals for the legs on the centre column, slip the bottom into a three-jaw chuck, gently squeeze, and the impressions will show the positions. Drill, insert dowels, and glue on the legs. A little rub with a file to the top end of the leg, to produce a slightly concave shape, will aid a nice snug fit round the curve of the column. Next, cut out a $1\frac{1}{2}''$ circle and shape it up to make the packer that sits between the legs and the top (see Figure 6) and glue it in place. All that remains is to glue the top to the drawer section, and the leg part underneath. Complete the piece with your desired finish and you have a table any dolls' house would be proud to own – Photograph 4.

PHOTOGRAPH 4. The finished Georgian drum table, $2\frac{1}{2}''$ high and $3\frac{1}{2}''$ diameter.

MENDLESHAM CHAIR

THE Mendlesham chair is a form of Windsor chair made in Mendlesham in Suffolk. It owes something to its curved-back brothers, and to both Suffolk, from whence come the balls, and Norfolk, for the rail back. It differs from the more usual form of Windsor chair in having the bow back replaced by a squarer back rail, and straight back standing rails. The finest examples have boxwood inlay to the back rails. This is a very elegant form of country chair and a welcome addition to any dolls' house.

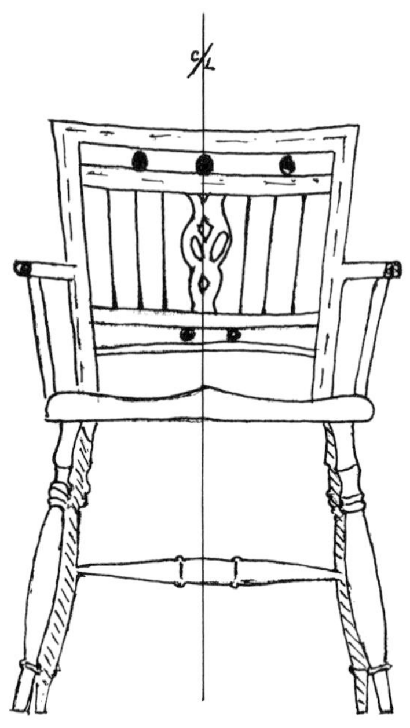

FIGURE 1. Front elevation.

TEMPLET FOR THE BACK

The first thing to tackle when making one of these chairs is the templet for putting together the back. All the measurements can be taken from Figure 1, and the only awkward part is hollowing out the base of the templet. As this is also the most important bit, it needs to be done with some care. Figures 2 and 3 show how it works, and you do have the compensation of knowing that once it is made, you will be in a position to turn out chairs for all your admiring friends!

TIMBER

So let's get going on a chair, or a pair if you prefer. I find that it is as easy to make a pair as it is to make just one. First we need to sort out what kind of timber to use. It needs to be a close-grained wood, and fairly hard, as it must be able to

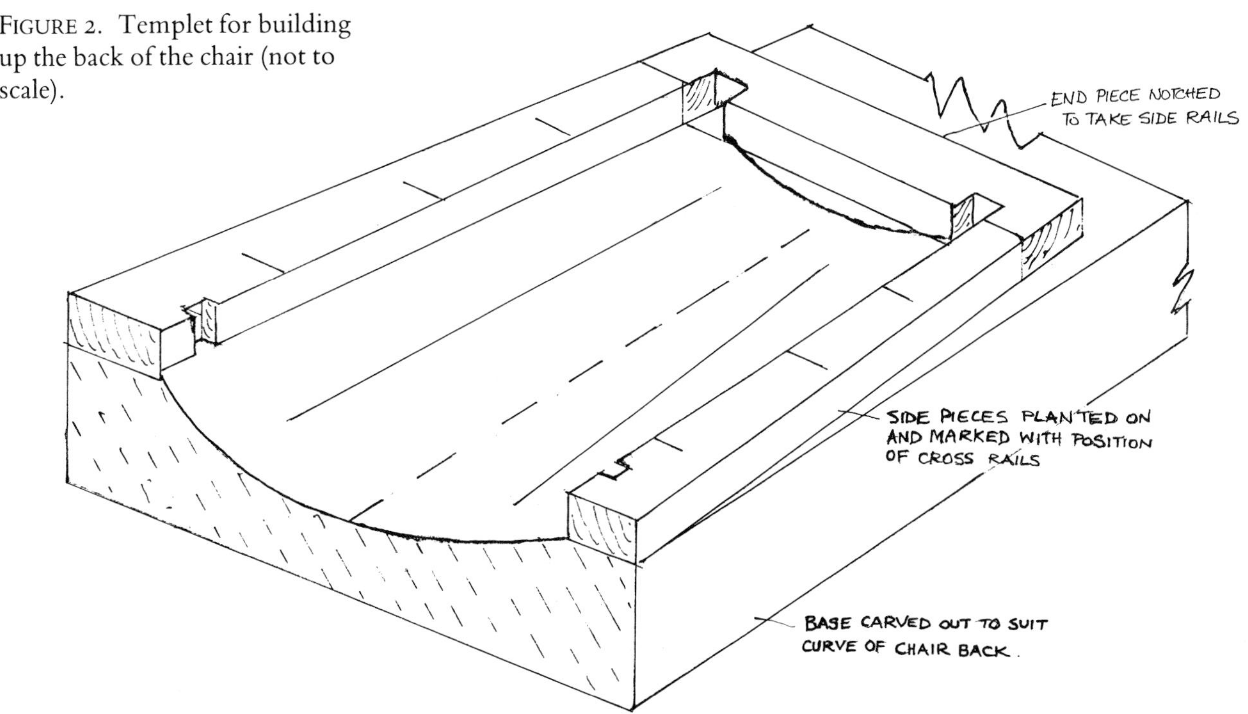

FIGURE 2. Templet for building up the back of the chair (not to scale).

hold a good edge to allow the legs to be turned. Something like beech, which will give you a light finish, or one of the fruit woods would be suitable. The real thing would have had a seat made of elm, but this tends to have too open a grain for miniature work. The chair illustrated was made from beech, stained and polished.

BACK

The first job is to prepare a piece of timber from which to make the back. This needs to be wide enough to allow the widest top rail to be cut from it, at least a couple of inches long, and thick enough to allow the curve of the back to be shaped into it. Figure 2 shows this much more clearly than words can describe. It is not too difficult to achieve using a half-round rasp and finishing off with glass paper. This is probably the most important part of the whole task, and while one would like to think that the curve would be exactly as per the drawings, it is probably more important that it should be the same as that of the templet.

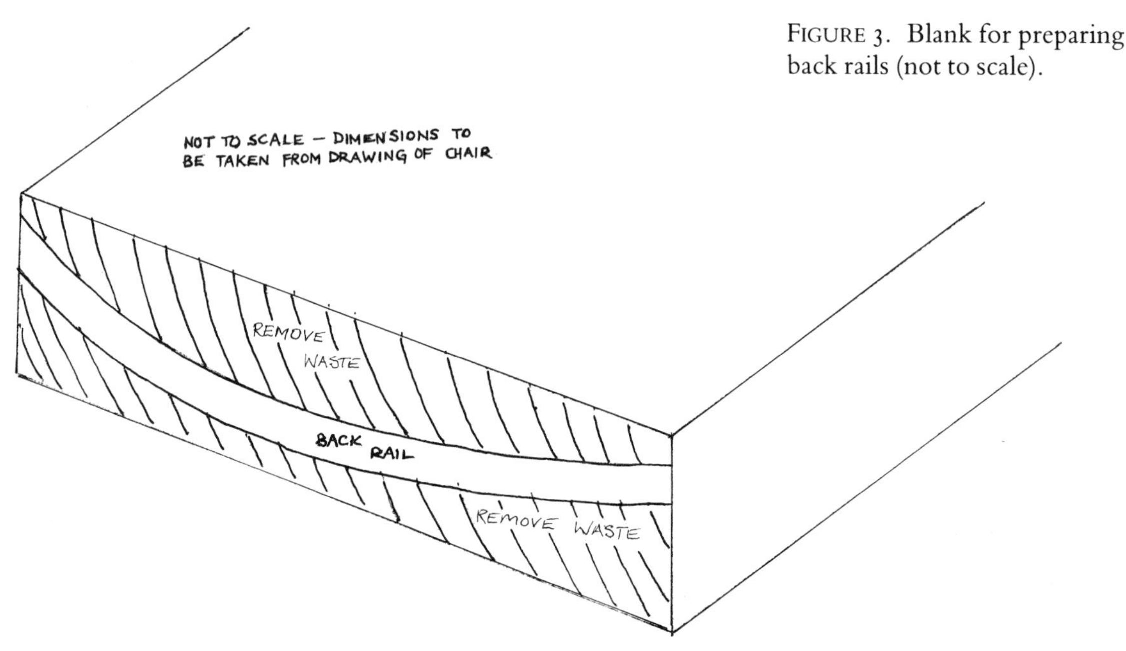

FIGURE 3. Blank for preparing back rails (not to scale).

SEAT

Now you can prepare a suitable piece for the seat. Either mark it directly from the drawing or, preferably, make a templet first as this makes it easier to mark the position for the legs. Cut out the shape of the seat. One of the features of Windsor-style chairs is the saddle-shaped seat, and this should now be done with a gouge, if you think you can cope, or more easily with a ball-shaped carborundum in a drill. It is probably as well to leave the drilling of the seat until the legs have been turned.

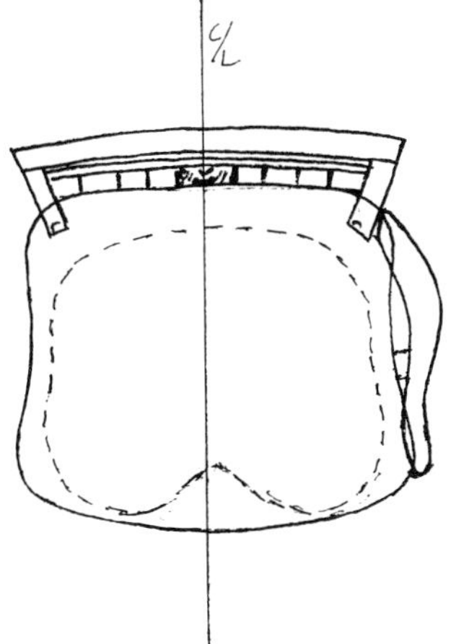

FIGURE 4a. Plan.

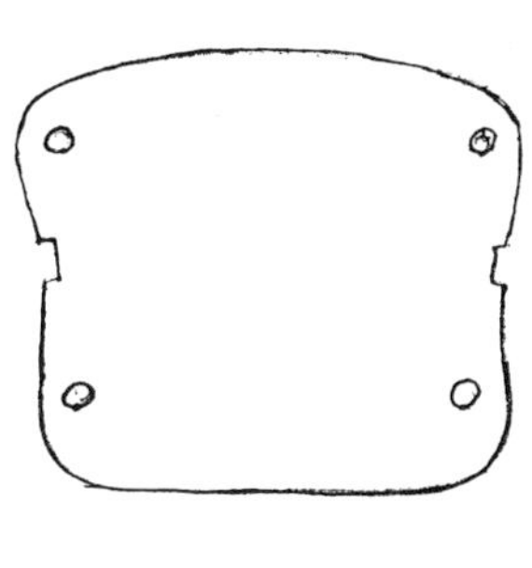

FIGURE 4b. Underside of the seat, showing position of holes for legs.

BACK RAILS AND SPLAT

The prepared timber for the back rails should now be sliced into pieces of the correct thickness, and the two straight pieces for the back side rails prepared and laid down the long sides of the templet, lodging them in the notches at the bottom. The top back rail goes right across, while all the others fit between the side rails. Before gluing these in place it is as well to cut and fit the two rails at the top and bottom of the slender infill rails. These should then be removed again and drilled to take the small rods, which in turn should be made with the help of the draw plate (see page 8), and the whole assembly glued into the templet. This leaves the centre splat to be made and fixed. As it is pierced quite a number of times, it is perhaps as well to make it from a piece of 1mm plywood.

BOTTOM RAIL AND BALLS

The bottom rail is not the same shape as the others, being rounded all along and fitted with a slight upward bend. The final part of this assembly is to put in the all-important balls. These can be made by cutting short sections of cocktail stick, and rolling them between two pieces of glass paper until they become round. They can then be glued in place. When the whole assembly is dry it should be gently extracted from the templet and set aside for the time being.

LEGS

Now is the time for a little bit of turning to make the chair legs. Prepare the timber, and take the shape of the legs from Figures 1 and 2. All you need to remember is to leave a little bit of extra length on the legs and cross rails to allow for fitting them into holes. Remember to drill holes in the legs for the cross rails before fitting the legs to the seat. It is difficult enough to make these small holes when you can hold things down, without making it even more difficult. You may find it easier not to try to turn the cross rails on the lathe, but to shape them by twisting them in a piece of glass paper held in the fingers. From your prepared templet (see Figures 4a and b) mark out and drill the holes in the seat for the legs. The holes should not go all the way through the seat, and at this scale it is easy enough to guess the angle and drill them by eye. Finally, glue the seat, legs and cross rails together and set aside to dry thoroughly.

PHOTOGRAPH 1. Turning the legs.

FIGURE 5a. Side elevation.

FIGURE 5b. Plan of arm.

ARMS AND ASSEMBLY

This leaves the final assembly and the attaching of the arms. The back as made up in the templet is deliberately over-long and should now be cut to the correct length, allowing enough for it to be let into the seat. Mark and drill the seat and glue in the back at the appropriate angle. Cut out the arms and uprights (Figures 5a and b), noticing that the uprights are notched into the seat. It helps to fix these with a small dowel as the arms tend to get knocked very easily. A small notch in the side back rails also helps to locate and fix the arm.

FINISH

As for the finish, the amount of gluing required in this model means that if a stained finish is required, it is probably better to stain all the separate pieces before putting them together, as it is very difficult to get stain to 'take' over the glue. Whatever finish you opt for, keep it light – no thick varnish please! The essence of this chair is that it must appear light and fragile while not being so.

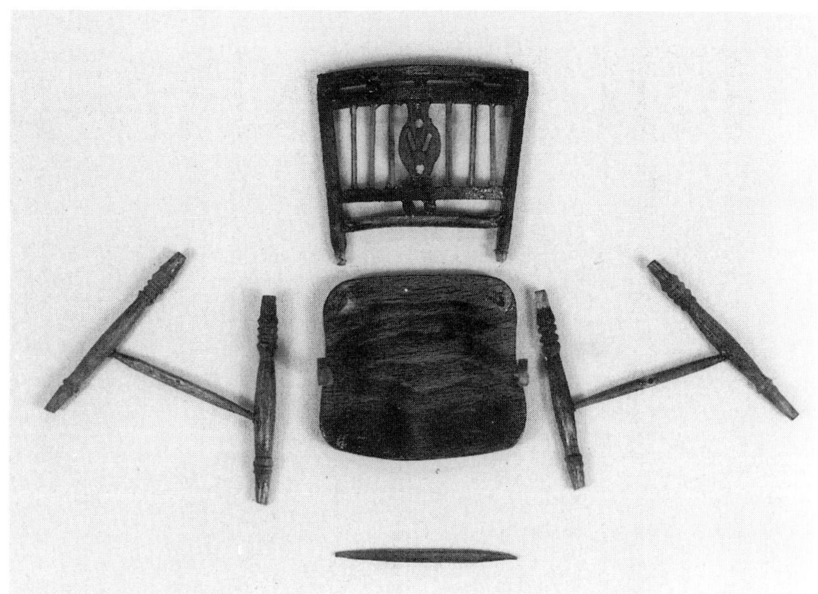

PHOTOGRAPH 2. The parts of the chair.

PHOTOGRAPH 3. The Mendlesham chair complete.

FOUR-POSTER BED

THE bed needs to be made from a fairly close-grained timber, and I used a suitable piece of oak from my own selection of secondhand pieces of furniture. If you do not have a usable piece of oak, it is possible to use any close-grained timber and stain the end result to look like oak.

HEAD AND FOOTBOARDS

The first step is to take two pieces of veneer or, better still, very thin ply about 1mm thick, and to cut them accurately and squarely to form the head and foot boards of the bed – see Figures 1 and 2. The real bed consists of a framework which is inset with carved panels. If you are a purist, you will make the model in the same manner. However, we will assume that you are one of us lesser mortals, and will stick an imitation framework on to the prepared panel. (Please do not misunderstand me: I agree that with certain pieces of furniture it is essential that everything should be done as in full-size practice. This, however, is intended as an easy exercise in making a bed for your own dolls' house, so we will do it the simple way.)

FRAMEWORK

Prepare your imitation framework from strips measuring approximately $\frac{1}{4}''$ by $\frac{1}{16}''$ thick, and $\frac{1}{4}''$ by $\frac{1}{8}''$ thick. You will need over 2 feet of the $\frac{1}{16}''$ and about 6″ of the $\frac{1}{8}''$. The $\frac{1}{8}''$ strips

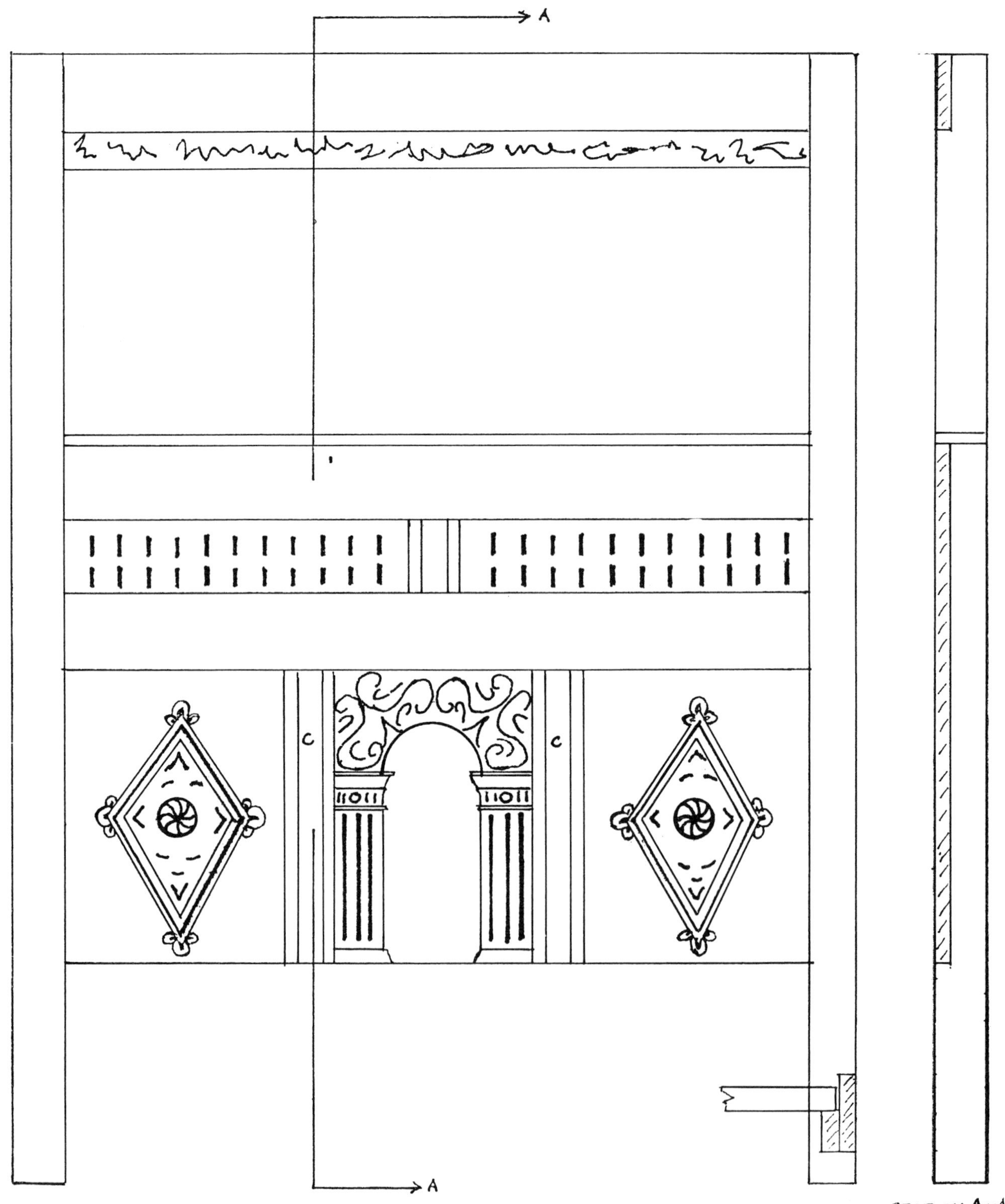

FIGURE 1. The headboard, showing section A–A.

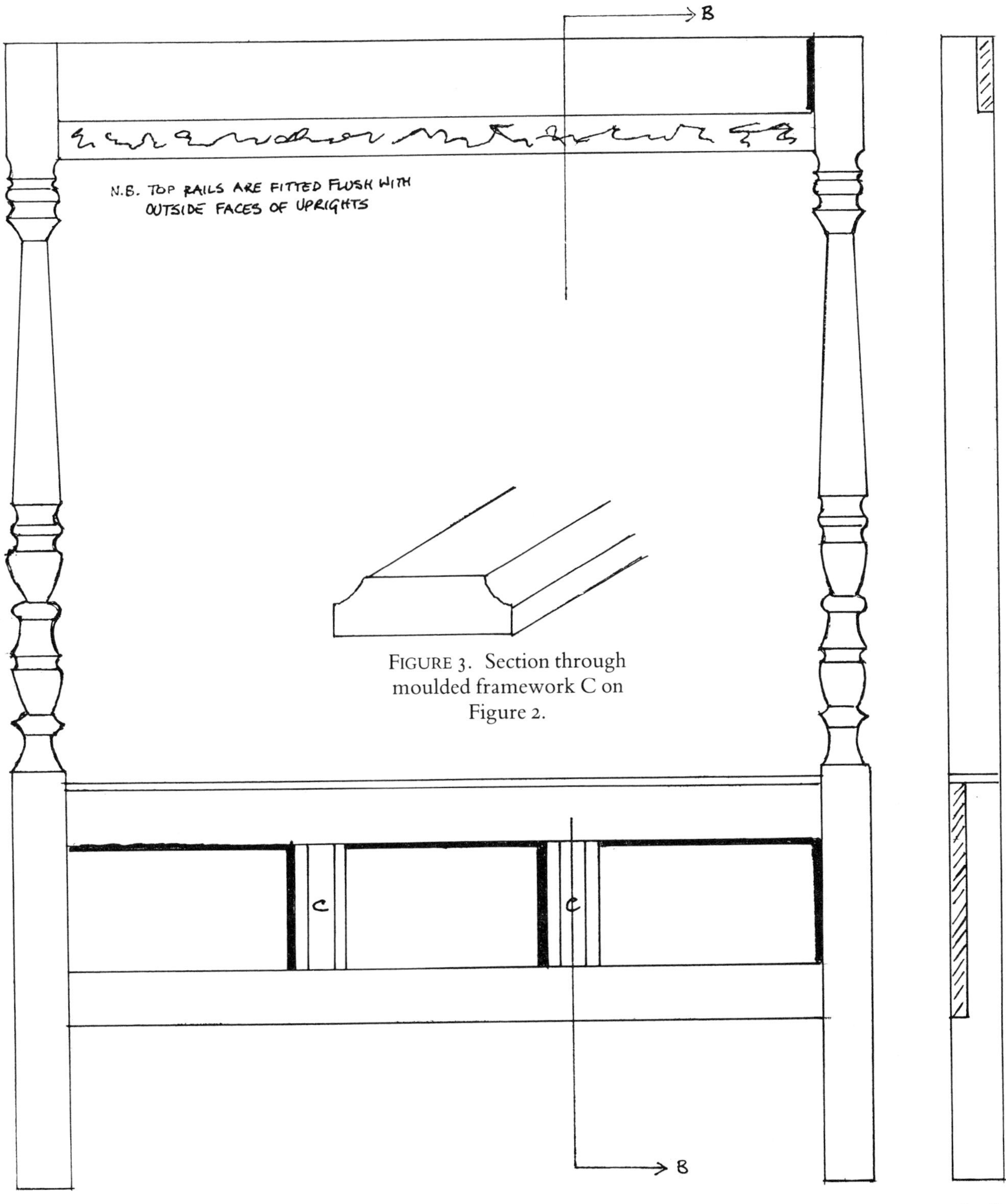

FIGURE 3. Section through moulded framework C on Figure 2.

FIGURE 2. The footboard, showing section B–B.

(marked C) need to be moulded as shown in Figure 3. (If you own a small router, it is very simple to do. Alternatively, you can use a small rebate plane or, even easier, buy some ready-moulded material.) Cut the pieces to length and simply stick them to the prepared head and footboards as shown in Figures 2 and 3. Do not fix the capping rail at this stage, as it needs to be a good fit between the uprights. Photographs 1 and 2 show the head and footboards.

PHOTOGRAPH 1. Detail of carved headboard.

PHOTOGRAPH 2. Detail of footboard.

CARVING

Now comes the interesting (and cheating) bit – how to do the carving that you can see on both the drawings, and especially Photograph 1, which covers the headboard. As with all my models, there is a hard way and an easy way to do this. The hard way is to get out your scalpel and all your miniature carving tools and get stuck into it, and jolly good luck to you.

The easy way is to take your soldering iron and indulge in a little old-fashioned poker work. If you have a removable bit to your soldering iron, it is a good idea to sharpen it to a chisel shape, so that even the most intricate of carving can be simulated. As the finished result is going to be stained, the overall effect is very realistic. The stain seems to run into the poker work and create an illusion of depth and age.

Having created your head and footboards, now stain them. If you leave it until later, glue will create an area of 'no go' for the stain. Set them aside and continue with the preparation of the four main uprights.

UPRIGHTS

The uprights are 4″ × 4″ full-size, i.e. just over ¼″ square to scale. The back ones are left square, but the front pair are turned between the height of the top of the footboard, and 9″ below the canopy – see Figure 2. The actual size of the uprights is 6½″ and the area to be turned is 3½″.

I am always being asked, 'Is a lathe really necessary?' I do think the answer has to be yes! I know there are those who can create wonders with a hand drill, but frankly they are few and far between. These days, as the price of miniature lathes is quite reasonable, it makes life so much easier and the job so much more pleasurable. The lathe does not have to be very complicated, so long as it revolves the work steadily and securely. It is surprising what can be done with a file and sandpaper, but *please*, as with all machine tools, watch it! Given half a chance, any machine tool will have

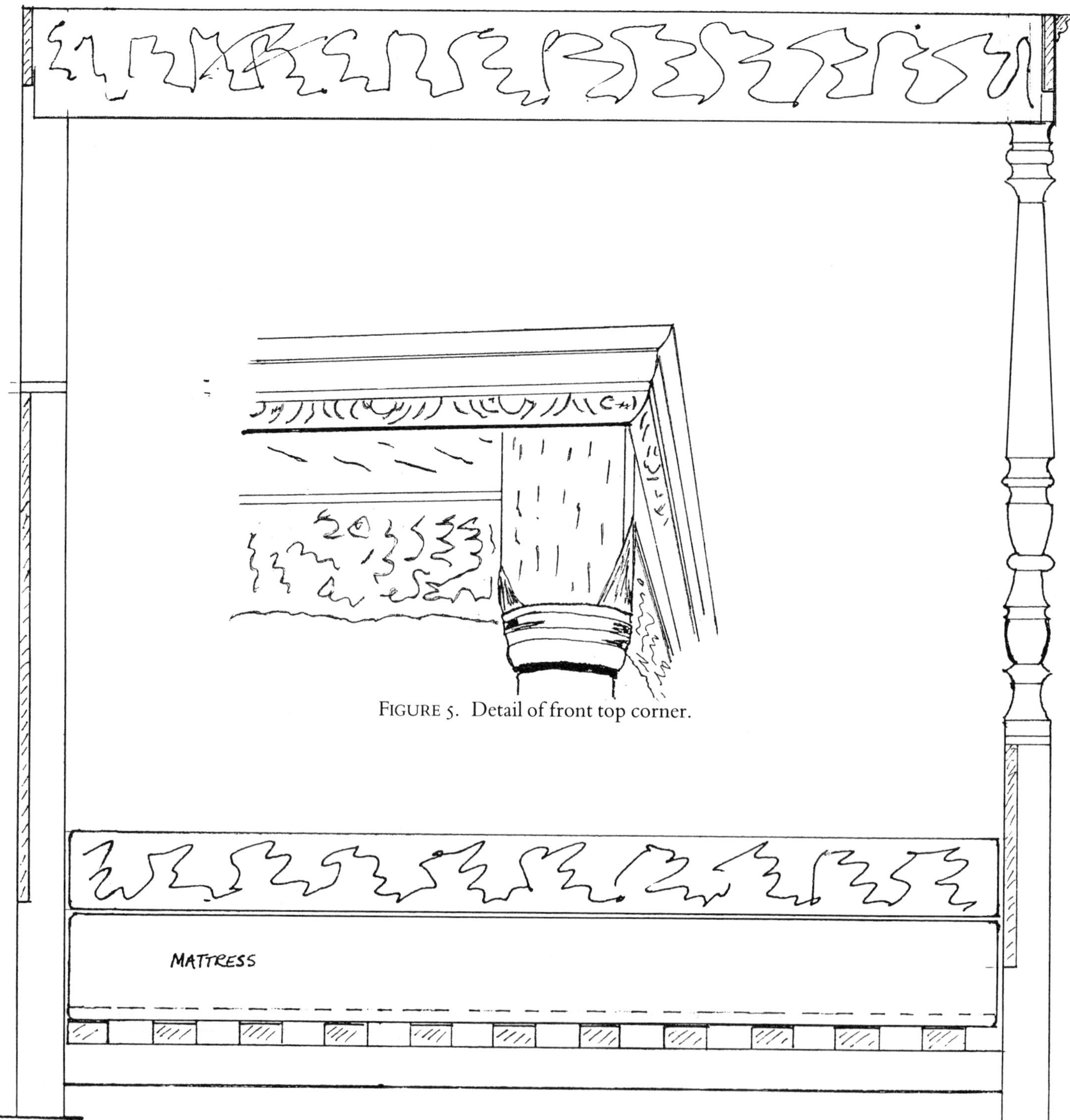

FIGURE 5. Detail of front top corner.

FIGURE 4. Sectional side elevation.

you. They all need to be treated with the greatest respect and even a small tool can give you quite a nip.

RAILS

Having completed and stained the four uprights, the next step is the making of the four side rails and the two top end rails – see Figure 4. These pieces are scaled 6″ × 1″ and you will require about 3 feet of it in all. Again, cut it carefully to length from Figures 1, 2 and 3, stain the pieces and leave them to dry.

ASSEMBLY

Now we can begin to put the bed together. Take the prepared headboard and the two square uprights, and lay them on a flat surface, together with the top end rail. You will now see the importance of making the headboard square!

You can rely solely on the strength of the glue to hold the pieces together, or you can fix them with small dowels made from cocktail sticks or bamboo. I think it is worth the extra effort of using dowels for the additional security it gives. Now do the same with the footboard and set it aside to dry. Figure 5 and Photograph 3 show what the corners should look like.

PHOTOGRAPH 3. Detail of top corner.

We now have a head and a foot that need to be fixed the appropriate distance apart with the four side rails (two top and two bottom).

I think the easiest way to do this is to tack a straight piece of timber to your building board and to use it as a register for the tops of the uprights and the top rail. I suggest you do the top first, as the bottom rail is, in fact, set up from the bottom of the uprights. With both rails fixed, reverse the bed and repeat the operation for the other side.

SLATS

To finish the framework of the bed, fix slats which will support the mattress. You will need to make an inner batten to the bottom rails (about half their height) and glue this to the inside of the bottom rails. The slats are then cut and fixed on top of this inner batten, leaving a small recess at the top to hold the lower mattress in place.

PHOTOGRAPH 4. The four-poster bed complete.

CANOPY

The canopy is made from material which should match one, or both, of the mattresses. The beauty of this method of making it is that you do not need to touch, or know anything about, needles and cotton. I use an iron-on gauze to produce all my hems, which gives a nice stiff piece of material. Cut it out and stick it with Copydex to the inside of the top rails, between the uprights, leaving about ¼″ below the rail.

Next, cover the whole top of the bed with the material, turn down the edges and stick them to the outside of the rails. The last job to be done on the bed itself is to fix a cover moulding to the outside of the top rail to cover the overhanging material of the top.

The mattresses are made from polyester foam of suitable thickness, covered with matching material and stuck with Copydex. The bottom one does benefit from a card base.

Sleep tight!

VICTORIAN SUMMER HOUSE

AND CROQUET SET

WHEN our Victorian ancestors were building their large houses and setting out the gardens, they nearly always included a summer house, some of which were quite bizarre affairs. Few, however, can have been built by one more illustriously named than he who constructed the one upon which the model is based, for inside the door is a brass plate bearing the following legend:

HENRY JULIUS CAESAR
RUSTIC HOUSE BUILDER
TO THE
QUEEN AND ROYAL FAMILY
KNUTS FORD CHESHIRE

After that, one can only follow with the replica of his masterpiece.

BODY

Figure 1 is a full-size plan of the base of the house. Use $\frac{1}{16}''$ plywood for this, and when marking it out, mark and cut out a second one in scrap hardboard, which will be used as a templet for constructing the roof. Some scale $3'' \times 3''$ floor joists at 18″ centres will help to stiffen up the floor. Cut the sides also from $\frac{1}{16}''$ plywood – these are again drawn full size in Figures 2 and 3. Note there are three sizes of sides: the ones which contain the windows and door, three in number, are all one size (Figure 2); four narrow panels are all the same (Figure 3), and the remaining panel, opposite the door, is made to fit the remaining gap to allow for any small accumulative error.

FIGURE 1. Plan of summer house floor and the 'former' for making the roof. For clarity the top rail to each section is omitted.

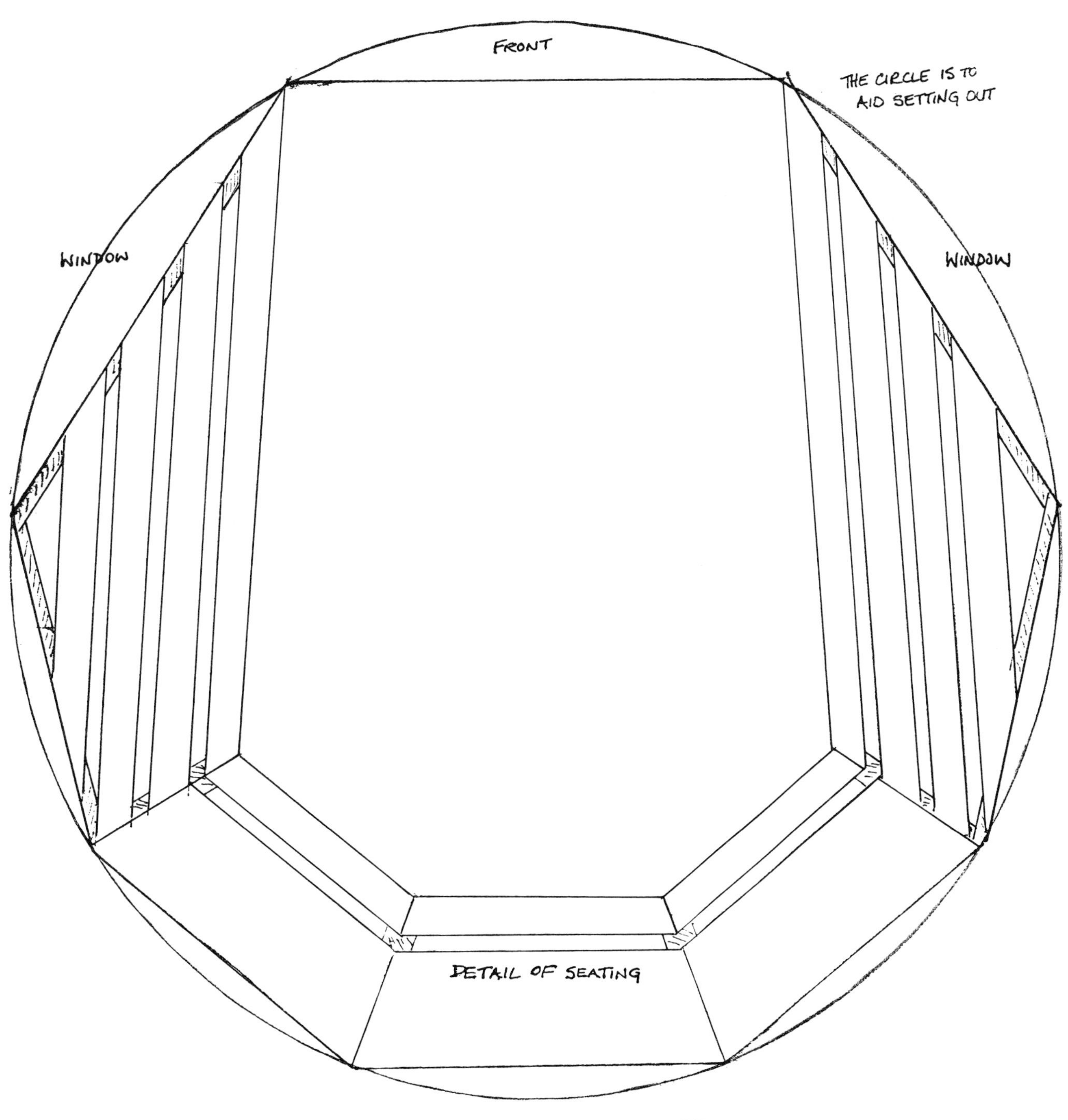

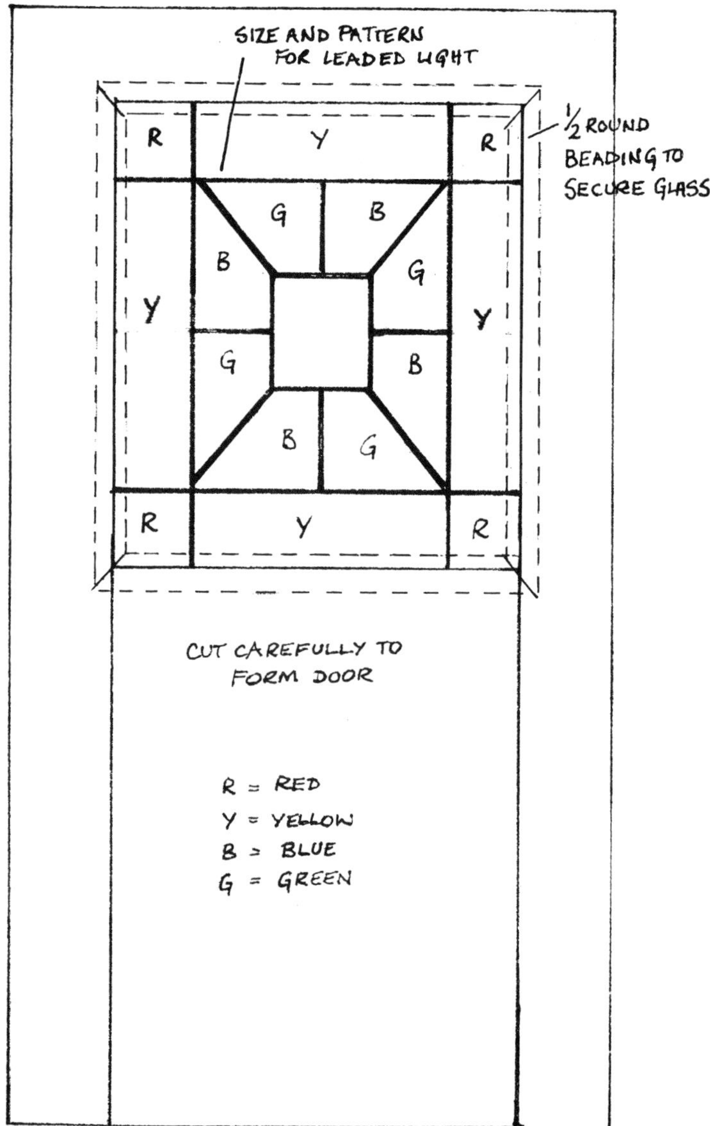

FIGURE 2. Elevation of large section of side, showing door and window. Cut three from $\frac{1}{16}''$ ply, two with windows and one with a door.

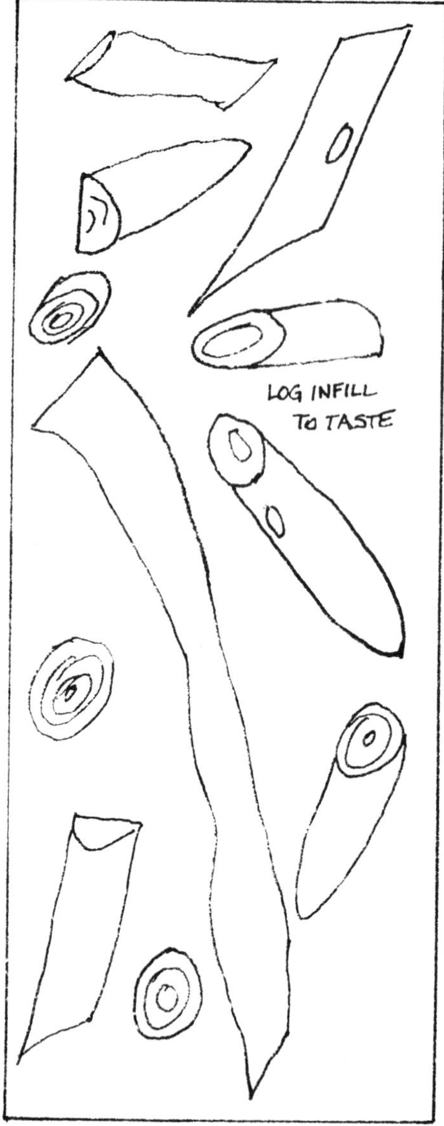

FIGURE 3. Elevation of small section of side. Cut four from $\frac{1}{16}''$ ply.

The windows and door should be cut out next. Either use a fret saw, or $\frac{1}{16}''$ plywood can be cut quite easily with a craft knife. Whichever you use, cut the top door corners as square as possible, as the cut-out will be used for the door and will require a window cut into it. Each section needs a piece of scale 2″ × 2″ glued top and bottom. The bottom rail should be set up $\frac{1}{16}$″ from the bottom of the side to allow it to act as a cover for the base proper.

All the sides can now be glued to the base, sanding each end of the 2″ × 2″ to the correct angle and gluing them to each other. Where the sides join on the outside of the building, rub with a piece of sandpaper to form a small flat, and glue a length of $\frac{1}{4}$″ dowel, with a similar flat planed on to it, down the length of the join. Photograph 1 shows the assembly to this point. It can now be stained to represent the creosote finish then put on one side while the roof is constructed.

PHOTOGRAPH 1. The basic structure.

ROOF AND DORMER WINDOW

I choose to make the roof as a separate item so that it will lift off. There is no reason why it should not be made as one entity, but access to the interior of the summer house would be quite difficult.

To make the roof, start with the second base that was cut from hardboard. In the centre, glue or fix a square piece of wood 4″ high. On top of this goes a round, tapered section ½″ high. The taper needs to be that of the angle formed by the rafters as they are glued to it. This tapered section is not glued to the top of the square, but is fixed so as to be removable, as it will eventually form the apex of the roof. The base stands on a second scrap base and is distanced ½″ from it. Photographs 2a and 2b show this clearly.

PHOTOGRAPHS 2a and 2b. Construction of the roof.

The eight rafters are scale 3″ × 3″ set on each angle of the base. Do not be tempted to square the angles to make the rafters fit more easily, or you will find that the completed roof will not! A small piece of double-sided tape will keep the feet of the rafters in place while the glue sets on the roof panels.

The eight roof panels are drawn out full-size, five as

PHOTOGRAPH 3. Make-up of inside of dormer window.

PHOTOGRAPH 4. Carcass of roof.

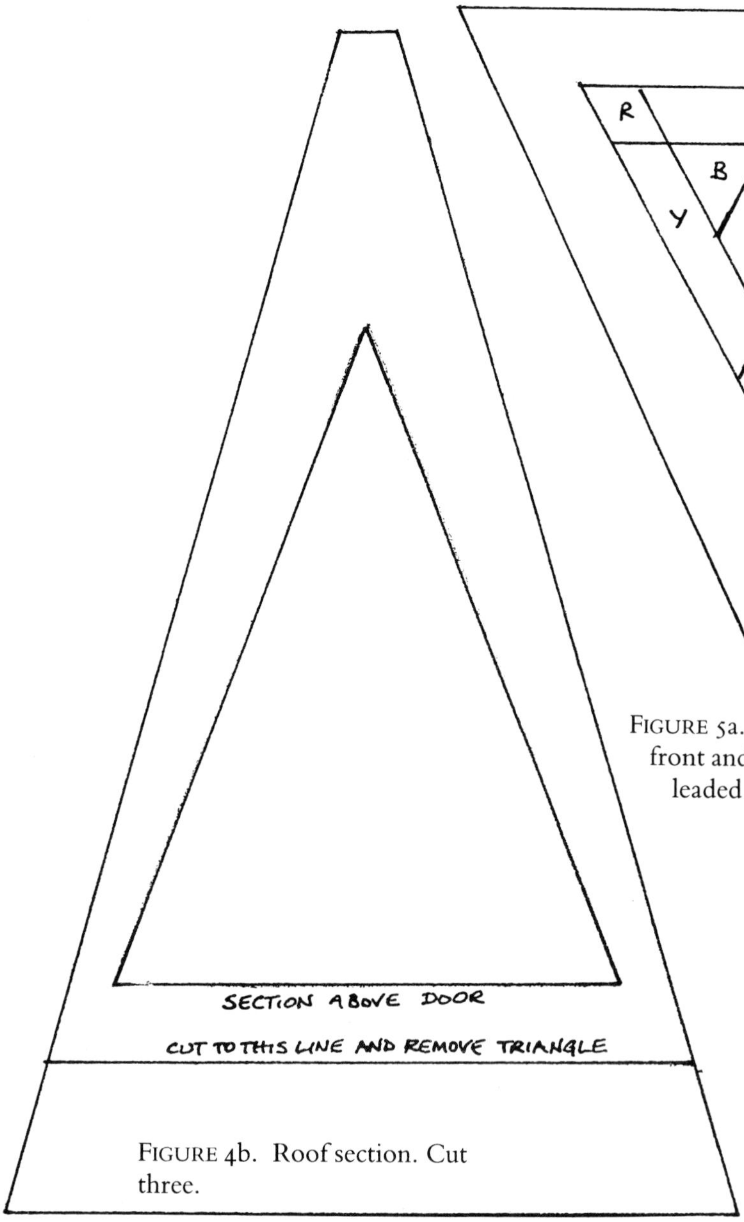

SECTION ABOVE DOOR

CUT TO THIS LINE AND REMOVE TRIANGLE

FIGURE 4b. Roof section. Cut three.

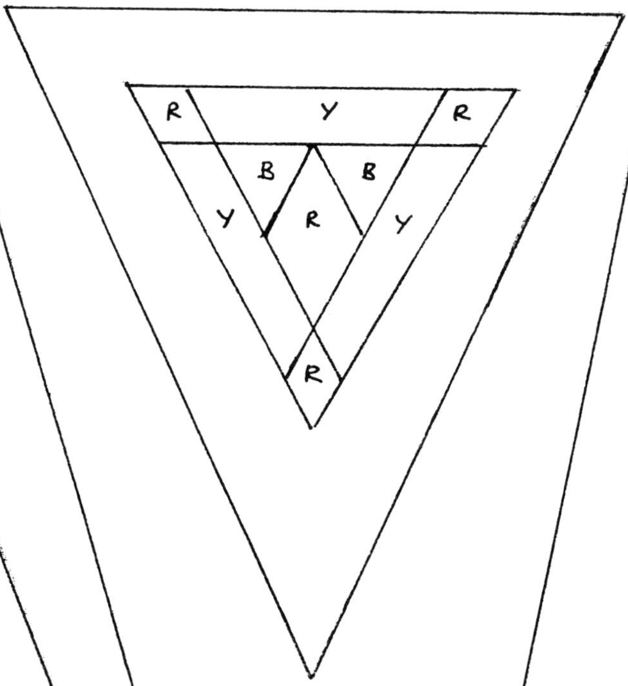

R Y R

B B

Y R Y

R

FIGURE 5a. Dormer window front and pattern for leaded light.

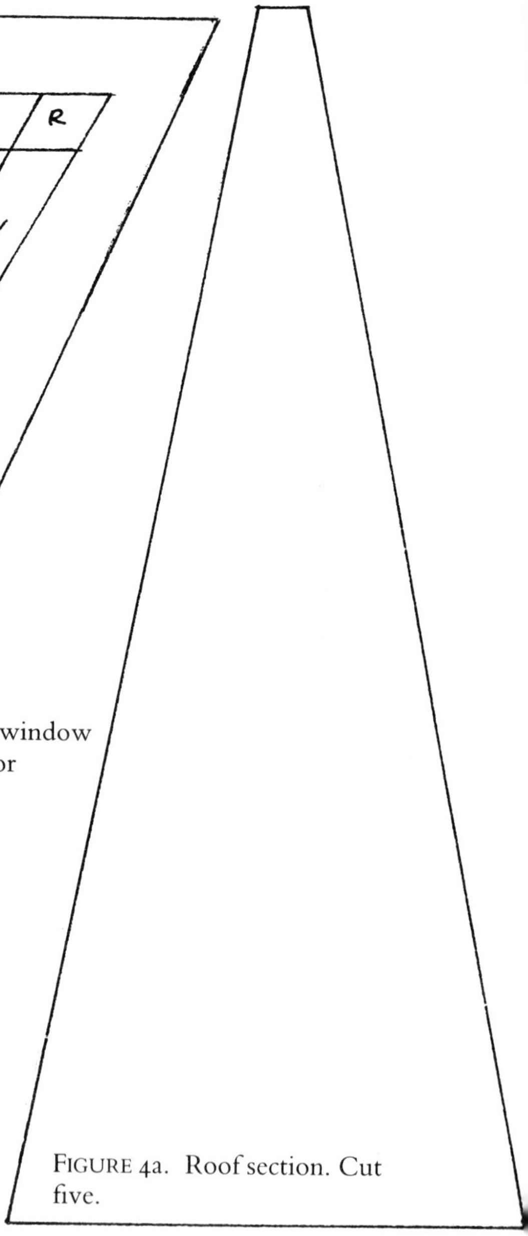

FIGURE 4a. Roof section. Cut five.

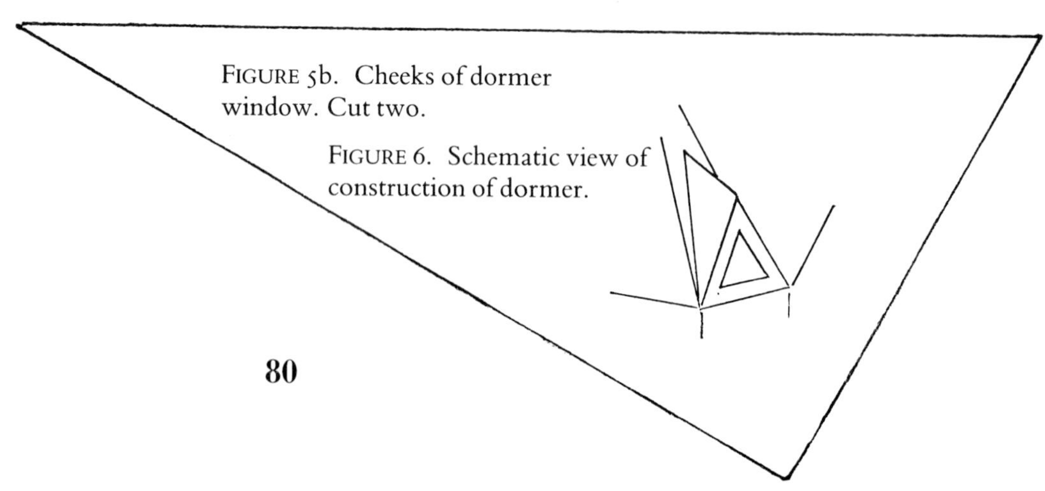

FIGURE 5b. Cheeks of dormer window. Cut two.

FIGURE 6. Schematic view of construction of dormer.

shown in Figure 4a, and three based on Figure 4b, the panel above the door being shorter and having the triangle removed. The panels and the cheeks and front of the dormer, also drawn out full-size (Figures 5a and 5b), should be cut from $\frac{1}{16}''$ plywood. Fitting is straightforward, the only slightly awkward part being the dormer, but Figure 6 and finished Photographs 3 and 4 show clearly how this is done. There is no need to take the corners off the rafters, but it may be necessary to use tape to hold the panels in place while the glue dries.

TILES

While the roof is still on the former is as good a time as any to fit the roof tiles. This is not difficult, but it is time-consuming and fiddly. The tiles should be made from $\frac{1}{32}''$ plywood cut into $\frac{1}{2}''$ squares. You will need about 450. You could use mounting board if you wish, but the thin plywood is not difficult to get – most good model shops keep it – and it can be cut with scissors (not the best needlework ones, or we will all be in trouble!)

To start the tiling, glue a course of tiles along the

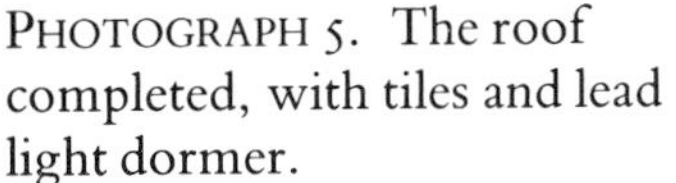

PHOTOGRAPH 5. The roof completed, with tiles and lead light dormer.

bottom edge of one of the roof sections. The tiles should butt up to each other and the end ones will need to be cut to match the angle of the section. Glue on the second course in such a manner that these tiles are butted in the middle of each tile below them, and they should just overlap the bottom row. It may be necessary to use some cut tiles in order to prevent the butts from being on top of each other. (If in doubt, look at any tiled or slated roof.) Work up each roof section, remembering that there will be less tiles in each course.

When all the sections have been covered, sand each angle between sections to a small flat and glue on a strip of $\frac{1}{16}''$ plywood to represent the cement and sand fillet on the original.

The full-size summer house would have had leaded light windows, but unfortunately only the one in the dormer has survived, so that is the pattern on which the others are based.

LEADED LIGHTS

There are several ways of imitating stained glass windows, and this to my mind is by far the easiest. Glass of $\frac{1}{16}''$ is widely available (or as the glass manufacturers will insist on calling it, 2mm), or you can use one of the glass substitutes. You will need a roll of Decra Led self-adhesive lead strip, and some of the same manufacturer's glass stain. The strip I find best is the $\frac{1}{4}''$ wide flat profile – it is a bit expensive but there is enough on a reel to make all the stained glass windows in a $\frac{1}{12}$th scale cathedral, maybe even two cathedrals!

Cut the glass to the size of the two window openings. The beauty of using $\frac{1}{16}''$ glass is that it will fit flush with the plywood sides and only requires a mitred half-round section glued on to fix it. Take a length of the lead strip and, without removing the backing, stick it down on a spare piece of glass with some double-sided tape. With a steel rule and craft knife slice it into $\frac{1}{16}''$ strips. You will find it will lift clear of its own backing, to be placed where required on the pane of glass, making up the pattern, see Figure 2. Try not to get more

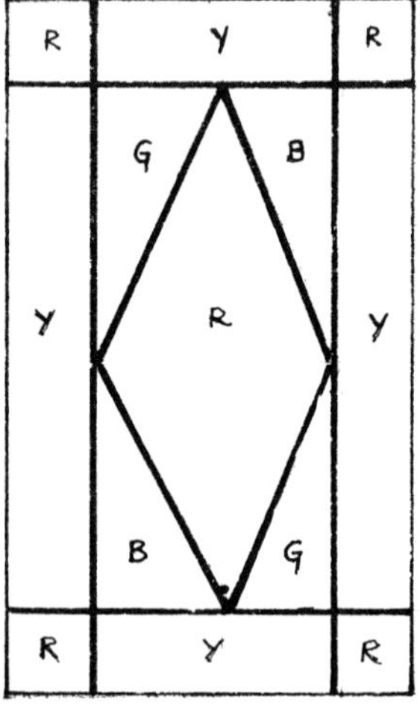

FIGURE 7. Pattern of leaded light in door.

than two pieces crossing. They look bulky and it is just as easy to butt the joins.

The strip will bend to a gentle curve, but if you need to make sharp bends, use one of the liquid solders from a tube. When all the strips are in position, it is a simple matter to colour the various shapes with the stains. Result – instant leaded lights. At the same time, make the windows for the dormer and the door, following Figures 5a and 7. You can now come back to the summer house, which you put aside to dry, and fit the windows.

INTERIOR

The next thing is to fit out the inside. The original has seating as shown in Figure 1, but I am sure that at some time it would have had lift-up lockers instead of the open benches. There is nothing difficult in reproducing the benches. They are 18″ high and sit on goal-post-shaped legs, with supports at each of the four rear angles, and bearers glued to the first two sections. Figure 1 and Photograph 6 show this in detail.

Above the seats, to a height of 4 feet, the walls were covered in wickerwork, and above that, including the roof,

PHOTOGRAPH 6. The inside of the summer house, showing a bird's-eye view of the seats.

was wallpaper on canvas. The remains of the original finishes are still visible on the walls of the prototype. The wickerwork has been simulated with a paper on the model.

EXTERIOR

One of the main features of the summer house is the treatment to the outside of the panels. This consists of shaped sections of log and branches, the biggest of which is about 5″ in diameter. On the model I have used prunings from our magnolia bush, but anything with a fairly smooth bark would be suitable. I found it easiest to cut the sections with a pair of secateurs, and for the longer pieces to cut a level surface with a chisel to allow them to sit flat at least in places. The main thing is not to overdo the number of pieces that you fix on.

The last thing to do to the summer house is to fix the door. It is a lot easier to use bought hinges than to make them yourself, and fitting the door follows the usual procedure. Half-round beading fixed to the door, as shown in Photograph 8, finishes the job.

PHOTOGRAPH 7. The exterior, complete with decoration.

PHOTOGRAPH 8. The finished summer house.

CROQUET SET

Having made the summer house, it automatically follows that you need a croquet set to go with it. The work involved in the house is far greater than that involved in the croquet set, but the reaction from viewers certainly does not reflect the difference. The drawings show all the pieces of the set. Figure 8 shows the pieces for playing with, and Figure 9 the parts of the box. The balls are made in the same way as for the Snooker Table (page 39), but this time from 8mm ball bearings. They are painted in the same way. The hoops are made from brass wire dipped in white paint. The mallet and smasher heads can be turned from any sort of hardwood, but they are actually available with square heads, so you could save on the turning. All the handles are made from bamboo barbecue sticks, as is the winning peg.

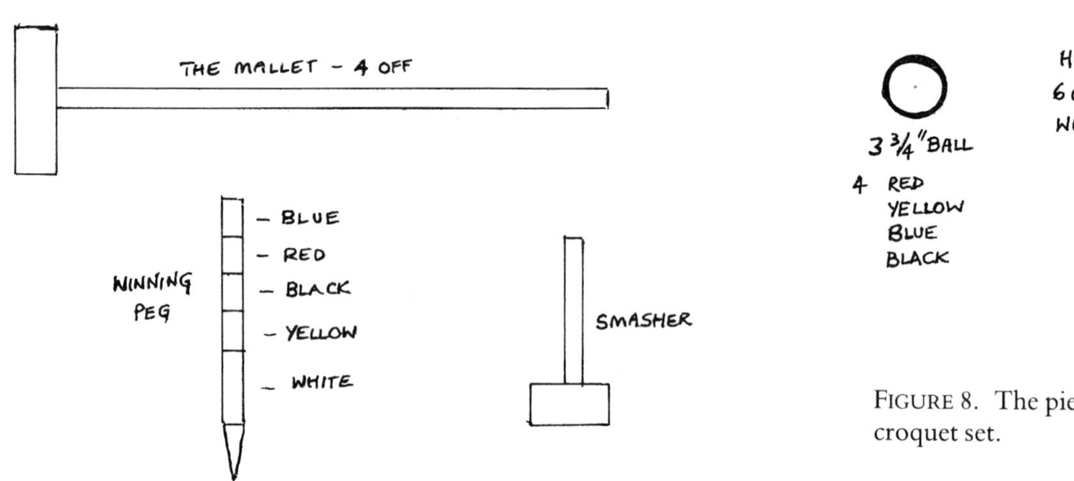

FIGURE 8. The pieces of the croquet set.

The box is made from $\frac{1}{32}''$ and $\frac{1}{16}''$ plywood, and the only point to note here is that the ends of the box go *inside* the bottom and sides. Fix a pair of hinges to the lid of the box and you are ready to go.

Even at this scale you will need an 8 feet by 6 feet table to play on. A pair of Victorian dolls preparing to play croquet would complete the picture.

PHOTOGRAPH 9. Turning the croquet mallet heads.

BOX SIDES – 2 OFF 1MM PLY

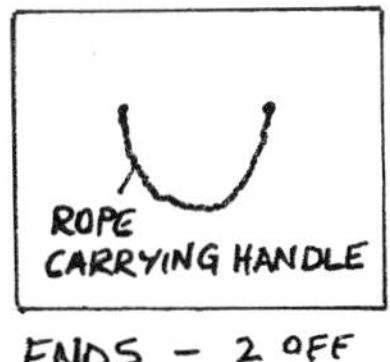

ENDS – 2 OFF
2MM PLY

TOP AND BOTTOM – 2 OFF 1MM PLY

FIGURE 9. The parts of the box.

PHOTOGRAPH 10. The entire croquet set.

SPINNING WHEEL AND STOOL

WHEN I decided to make a model of a spinning wheel, I knew very little about such things. Indeed, I was not even very sure about how a spinning wheel worked, but I was lucky enough to be able to photograph and measure the one in my local museum. This, along with some research at the public library, sorted out how the thing worked. For those of you who are as bemused as I was, I will try to explain as we go along.

PHOTOGRAPH 1. The original wheel.

WHEEL

The piece to start with is the actual wheel, the construction of which is completely different from any other type of wheel. For a start, the rim is in four pieces, which can be traced from Figure 1 and some patterns made. For the model illustrated I used yew, a wood from which the finest spinning wheels were often made. Prepare the wood to the correct thickness (see Figure 2), and mark out and cut the wheel rim segments. Leave some spare on the two biggest pieces to enable them to be screwed to the block on the lathe faceplate (see Photograph 2). The four segments now need to be glued up to form a rough circle, but as the rim has to be turned, it really is necessary to use something more than just glue to hold it together. The one shown in the photograph is put together with loose tongues glued in, and this requires the use of a router or fine slitting saw to form the grooves for the loose tongues. If you do not have the equipment to do this, you can put the segments together with dowels.

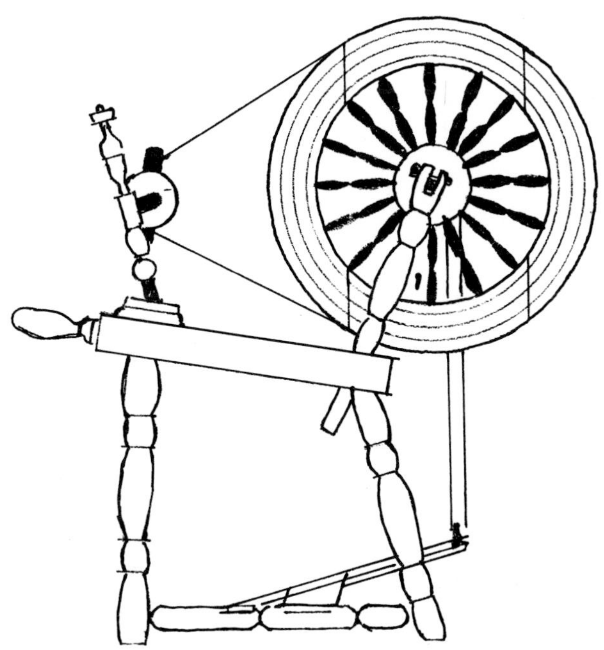

FIGURE 1. Side elevation.

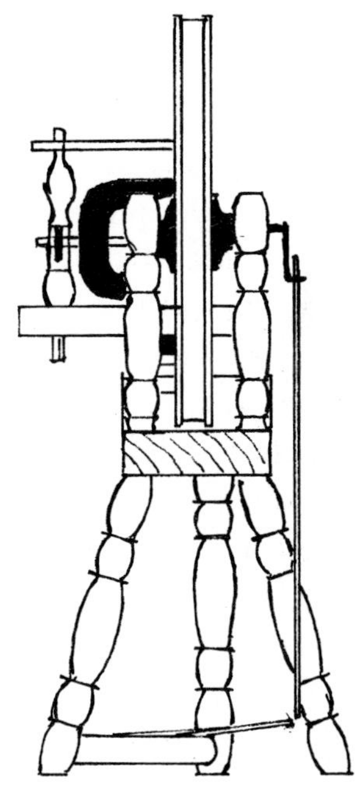

FIGURE 2. End elevation.

PHOTOGRAPH 2. Ready for turning the wheel rim.

Obviously, this is a project for which the use of a lathe is practically essential. I am sure that there are people who could, and will, produce it without, but for us lesser mortals a lathe makes life much easier. Screw a 1″ blank softwood disc to the faceplate, mark the centre, remove it from the lathe and fit the rim so that it runs as near as possible on the right line and certainly so that there is enough material to turn the inner and outer diameters to their correct sizes. Face up the front of the rim, turn the inside diameter true, and remove the piece from the faceplate. Now turn down the outer part of the 1″ blank disc to form a spigot which is a tight fit to the inside of the rim. Replace the rim, reversed, face the second side, and mark the outer diameter of the rim. Remove it again and cut away the spare timber to the line of the outer diameter. Replace it on the lathe and turn the outside diameter, and also form the rebate in the rim for the drive lines to run in.

The next job is to prepare the centre hub of the wheel. To allow the spokes to go into the wheel, the hub must be a split type (Figure 3). Chuck a suitable piece of timber, turn the outside diameter of the hub, and part off. Rechuck and bore the centre to take a $\frac{1}{16}$″ brass tube. With a razor saw, cut the hub in half through its thickness, so that you have two

FIGURE 3. Detail of split hub (not to scale).

circular pieces of wood with a hole through the middle. As you can see from Figure 3, this wheel has a total of sixteen spokes. The original wheel actually has eighteen, but drilling eighteen holes in the centre of a timber hub is very difficult. Sixteen is bad enough, and it would be a lot easier if there were only twelve or fourteen, so you can make up your own mind, but less than twelve might look odd.

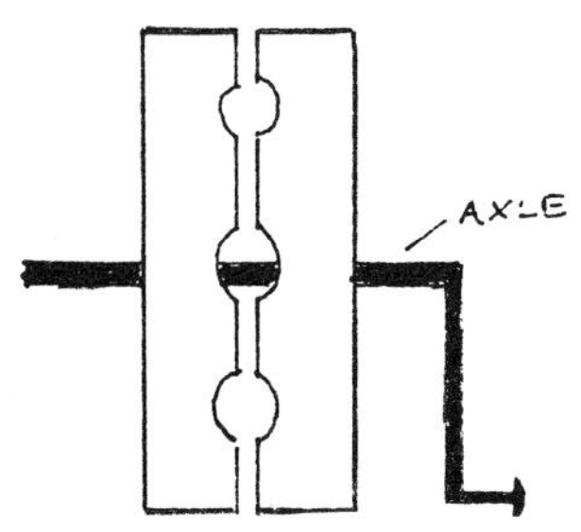

FIGURE 4. The hub, made from two separate pieces, showing the axle.

Ideally, the next step requires an indexing attachment. It is possible to make up one, as there are only these few holes to drill, or it is also feasible to measure and mark the hub where it needs drilling. Whichever method you use, clamp together the two parts of the hub and drill the holes along the line of the join, see Figure 4. These holes will need to be much finer than the size of the spokes or you will break the hub. This leaves the task of making the holes in the rim for the outer ends of the spokes. If you have a dentist's style drill, i.e. one that can drill at right angles, all well and good, otherwise you may care to try the folowing: cut a strip of 1mm ply equal to the width of the rim; fit it to the inside of the rim, remove it, measure the length of the strip, divide by the number of spokes, mark the positions, and drill holes to suit the ends of the spokes; fix the drilled strip to the inside of the rim.

The final job is to assemble the whole wheel. To do this it is necessary to jig the rim and hub in position as accurately as possible. Draw out the wheel full size on a scrap piece of timber, drill the centre the same size as the hub, and recess half the hub into the scrap wood to keep the spokes central. The hub can be held in position with a short length of $\frac{1}{16}''$ tube, and the rim with pieces of double-sided tape. The spokes can now be fitted and glued into the holes in the rim, and into the half hub. When all the spokes are in, glue on the second half of the hub. You have now completed the most difficult part of the project.

BASE BLOCK

One of the most attractive things about spinning wheels is the lovely names of the parts: mother-of-all, maiden, flyer.

However, the first part needed has a much more mundane title – it is the 'base block', the dimensions of which can be taken from Figures 2 and 5. At this stage you must decide whether to make all the parts work, as in the real article, or to glue them up as you go along. The spinning wheel pictured is made to come to pieces, and in theory, at least, would spin if you could find a raw material fine enough.

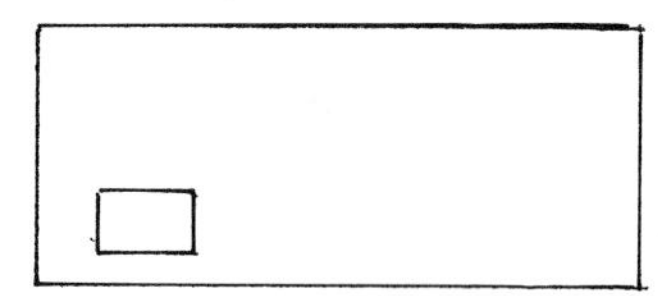

FIGURE 5. Plan of the base block.

In the base block, cut the rectangular hole to take the adjuster. The purpose of the adjuster is to put tension on the drive lines from the wheel to the flyer and bobbin. It consists of a block, with a hole and thread in it into which a screw goes. By turning the handle on the end, the mother-of-all is moved. To do it in this scale, use a small nut and bolt. Glue the nut to the wooden block, which in this case becomes a pin as well to carry the mother-of-all. Turn down the end of the bolt and fit a wooden handle. Make a collar to cover the hole in the base block.

LEGS AND WHEEL SUPPORTS

Now is as good a time as any to produce the turned legs and wheel supports. These are all quite straightforward and the sizes can be taken from Figures 1 and 2. Remember to allow enough on the length to fit into the base block. Note that the wheel supports go right through, and when you drill the holes in the base for them, take care that both holes are at the same angle. When gluing the legs in position, the single back leg, in addition to being longer, is positioned over to one side to avoid the tensioner – see Figure 2. The splay of the front legs, and exact position of the rear one, is quite critical, otherwise the wheel will have a tendency to fall over. Slots need to be cut into the top of the wheel supports to carry the wheel axle (Photograph 1 shows this clearly).

SPINNING MECHANISM

This brings us to the section of the spinning wheel for which all the other parts exist: the actual spinning bit. This consists

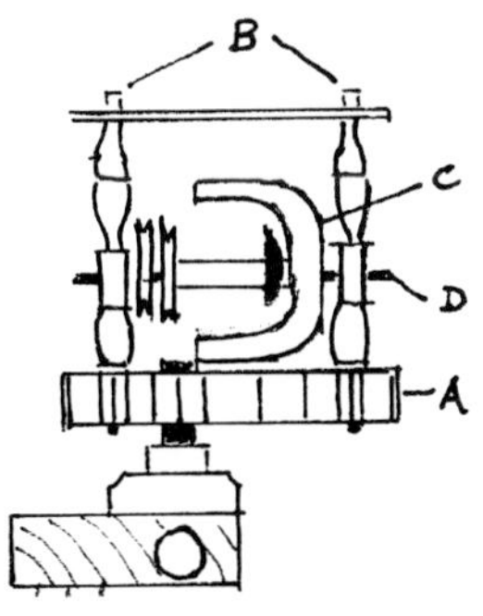

FIGURE 6. Flyer and bobbin.
A = mother-of-all; B = maidens;
C = flyer; D = bobbins.

of a flyer, with its detachable drive wheel; a bobbin, free running on the flyer shaft; and all the pieces to support them, Figure 6. The first piece to make is the mother-of-all, which is simply a turned piece of wood with three holes in it – one to take the pin from the adjuster, the other two for the maidens, which in turn support the flyer (see Photograph 4 of the original wheel for the arrangement). Figure 1 indicates that the pin from the adjuster is at an angle, and all the holes in the mother-of-all are at the same angle. You may find it easier to make the pin straight and vary the angle of the holes. Now turn the two maidens so that they will fit into the mother-of-all. They are made to be removable so that the flyer can be taken out and the bobbin changed.

PHOTOGRAPH 3. The model, showing the mother-of-all, maidens, flyer, bobbin and wheel supports.

The flyer (see Figure 7) is a horse-shoe shaped piece of wood fixed to a shaft. It has a drive pulley at one end, and the hollow fitting through which the wool passes is at the other. The drive pulley is made to unscrew so that the bobbin can be slipped off and changed.

When making the flyer, choose a piece of close-grained timber and drill the hole for the shaft before attempting to

PHOTOGRAPH 4. The mother-of-all, maidens and flyer on the original wheel.

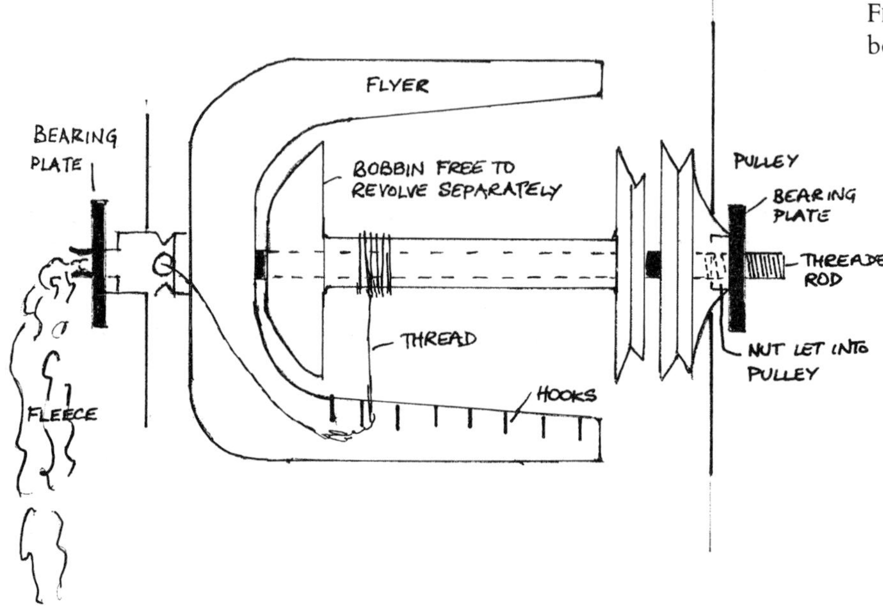

FIGURE 7. Detail of flyer and bobbin (not to scale).

cut it out. You may find this a very frustrating piece to make. My workshop was strewn with the remains of five abortive attempts before I got it right, so do not despair. Use a piece of $\frac{1}{16}''$ tube for the shaft and turn up the bobbin to be a loose fit on this shaft. This is the one part of the model which departs from reality. This is because the bobbin is slipped on to the flyer shaft and the drive pulley *glued* into place, instead of being fitted with a nut and screwed on. I justify my cheating by telling myself that, in any case, there is only one bobbin!

The shaft, where it projects from the back of the flyer, should be left to fit the bearing attached to the maiden (again see Figure 7). At the other end, cut off just beyond the bobbin and glue in a piece of $\frac{1}{32}''$ brass wire to fit the other bearing. This has the added advantages of distinguishing the two maidens. The bearing plates need cutting and filing from a piece of brass sheet. File a spike on one end of the shaft and fit it into a hole drilled in the maiden. You can now assemble the whole lot – and probably find, as I did, that I had drilled the hole in the mother-of-all in the wrong place, and that the drive pulleys did not line up with the main wheel. A mother-of-all joined five flyers in the scrap box! The final job for this part is to turn and fit the keeper rod to the top of the maidens.

TREADLE

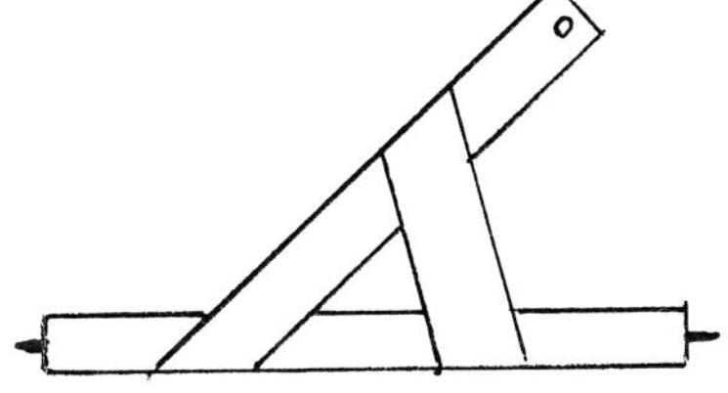

FIGURE 8. Plan of treadle (check measurement on model).

The last part of the spinning wheel is the treadle, the general shape of which is shown in Figure 8. The exact dimensions need to be taken from the model, as they will depend on the rake and length of the legs. The wheel needs to have a shaft with a crank at one end, see Figures 2 and 4. We already have a length of $\frac{1}{16}''$ tube through the hub, and this should be cut off close on either side and a length of $\frac{1}{32}''$ wire glued in and shaped to form the crank.

STOOL

All that now remains is to give the poor old spinner something to sit on. Even that is no luxury item, consisting simply of a seat, four legs and a back, as shown in Figure 9a, b, c and d. The one in Photograph 5 only has a chamfer on the edges of the seat and back, but they were frequently elaborately carved. I doubt this made them any more comfortable, but why not carve yours and make it more personal?

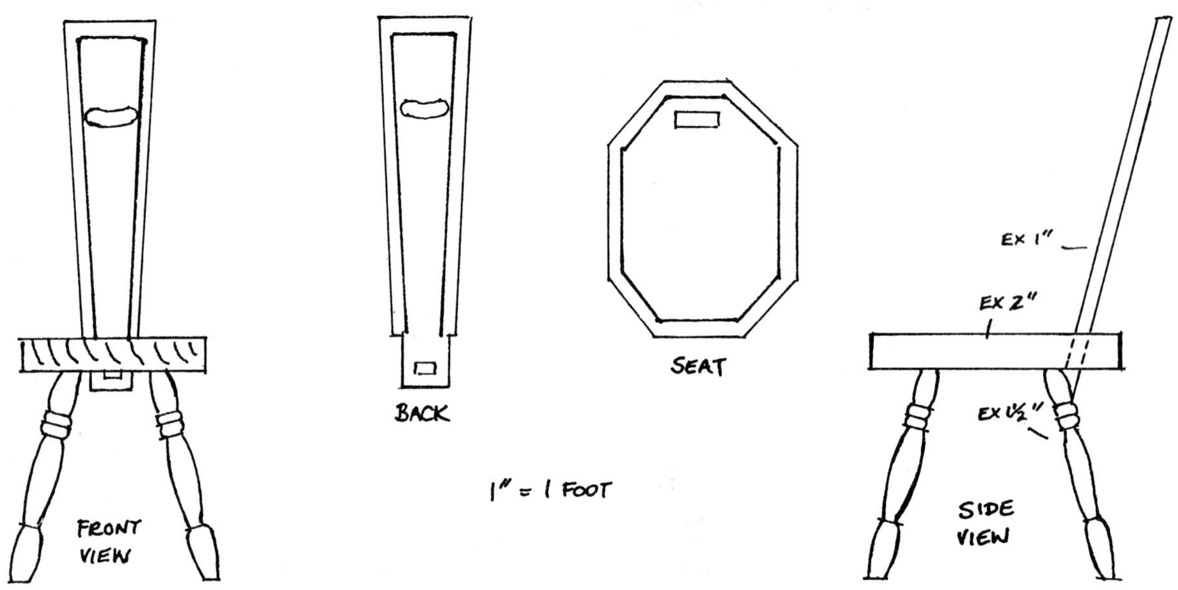

FIGURES 9a, b, c and d.

PHOTOGRAPH 5. The miniature Arkwright spinning wheel.

SHIP'S WHEEL

I AM not all that sure that a ship's wheel comes under the heading of 'furniture', but it certainly is unusual. The wheel described here was inspired by a photograph of one on a barge in Ipswich wet dock in summer 1987, and by personal memories from longer ago than I care to remember, when I spent many hours behind one on a real ship. The model is attached to a telemotor column, and mounted on a section of deck, complete with grating. This is because I do not have a dolls' house with walls on which to hang it (but an old pub with a nautical flavour would be suitable).

PHOTOGRAPH 1. The ship's wheel with deck and grating.

WHEEL

The construction of a ship's wheel is, again, completely different from that of any other wheel. In a ship's wheel the spokes go right through the rim, instead of being set into it, as is more usual. This being so, the obvious place to start is with the spokes. For the example, I used teak, which is not an ideal choice as it is inclined to be open-grained and does not take kindly to being turned to a fine finish. The piece I had, however, was fine-grained, and with patience it turned out well (no pun intended). The only problem with turning the spokes is that parts of them have to be left square (see Figures 1 and 2), and this creates a slight problem when holding them in a three-jaw chuck. The best solution seems

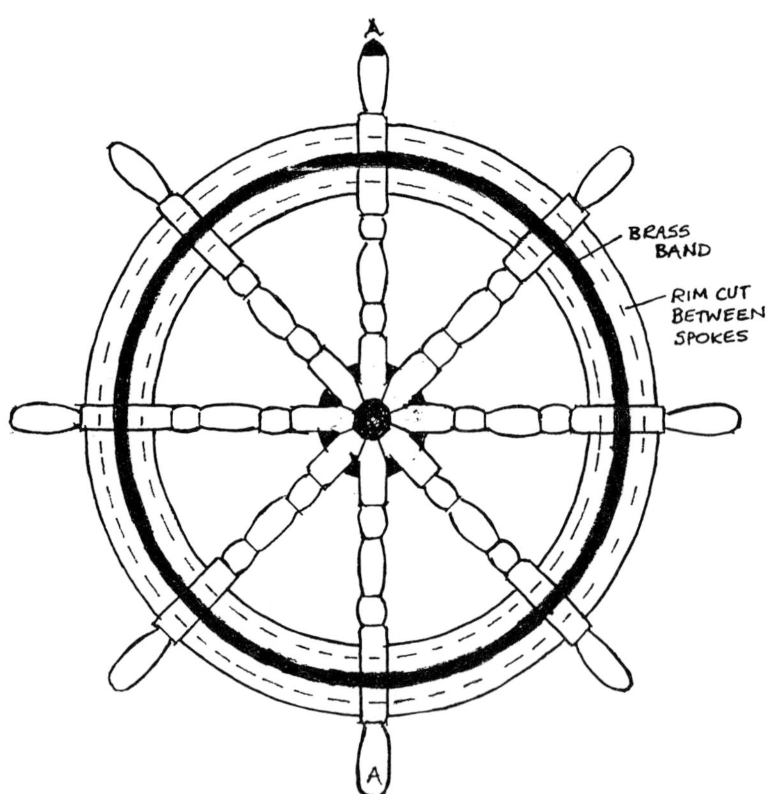

FIGURE 1. Front elevation.

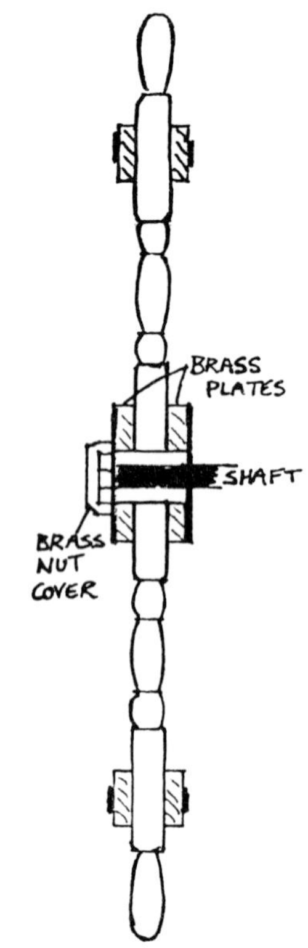

FIGURE 2. Section A–A.

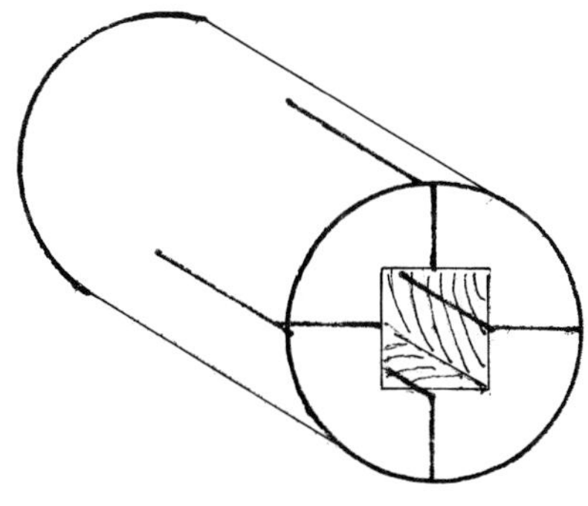

FIGURE 3. Holder for square end spokes.

to be one suggested to me by a friend, and that is to make up a holder from a piece of dowel, Figure 3. Drill a hole in the dowel slightly smaller than the square of the spoke. Square this circular hole, and saw the end with a slit saw to form a collet. Be sure that when the hole is drilled in the piece of dowel, it is held in the intended chuck, so that it is truly central. Turn all eight spokes, taking the measurements from Figures 1 and 2.

The hub in the real wheel is usually a casting with square holes for the spokes to fit in. In the model it is more practical to turn the hub and to drill the holes for the spokes. This means that the ends of the spokes will have to be rounded, and not left square, as shown in the drawings. At the same time, drill through the centre of the hub to allow for fixing a shaft. Now lay out the spokes and hub on a scrap piece of timber or hardboard. It helps if you cut a recess for the hub to allow the spokes and rim to lie in the same plane. It will also help if we use our old friend the double-sided tape to hold the spokes firmly in position.

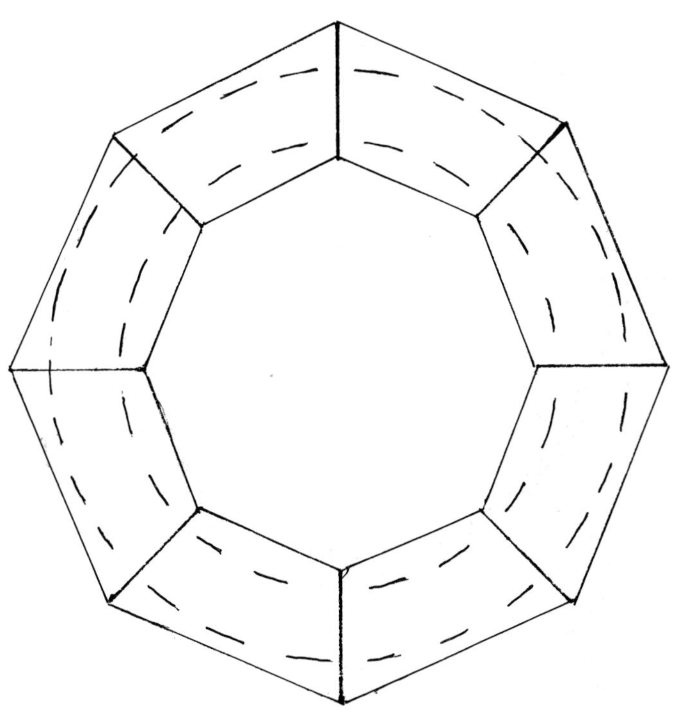

FIGURE 4. Setting-out details for the rim of the wheel.

The next step is probably the only tricky part of the job – turning the rim. On another scrap piece of wood draw the shape of the rim (from Figure 1). Cut eight pieces of timber of the correct thickness and wide enough to make each section (see Figure 4). Cut them at the required angle and butt glue on the drawing. On this occasion glue only! Later you will need to break these joints again. Remove the now octagonal rim and fix it on to the lathe faceplate (Photograph 2). Use double-sided tape, and for extra security, screw it at the joints, but drill first! You can now turn the inside, the outside, and one face. Reverse the rim and turn the other face. You will now have the completed, turned, and shaped rim, which you must now break at the glued joints. The next step is to cut and fit each section of the rim between the spokes and glue them into place – see Photograph 3 (it really is much easier than it sounds).

To add strength to the segmented rim, a further ring of wood is fixed to either side of the wheel. These are frequently made up in quadrants, and this is probably the easiest way to do it. Following the broken line in Figure 1, mark out and cut the eight quadrants, and sand, fit and glue four of them in place as the wheel still sits on its setting-out board.

PHOTOGRAPH 2. The wheel rim segments set up ready for turning.

PHOTOGRAPH 3. The segments of the rim fitted between the spokes.

The finishing touch to any ship's wheel is the brass ring that runs around the rim, and also adds considerably to the strength. Making it using the following method is a bit expensive, but still seems to me the easiest way. Cut two squares from 15thou brass sheet, each large enough to allow the rim to be cut in one piece. Screw a square to a piece of wood fixed to the lathe faceplate in the four corners – see Photograph 4. With a very sharp 'V' tool, cut the inner

PHOTOGRAPH 4. Preparing to cut the brass ring.

PHOTOGRAPH 5. Wheel with rim fitted, reinforcing quadrants and brass rim.

diameter and remove the centre. Now start the cut for the outer diameter. I found that it was easiest to turn the lathe by hand to cut these rings. Having cleaned up the ring and glued it in position, release the whole wheel, turn it over, and fit the wooden quadrants and brass ring to the other side. Lastly, turn a brass dome to seal the shaft hole (Figure 2).

If you are just making the wheel to hang on the wall, the job is complete apart from finishing with a couple of coats of teak oil, and you can start thinking about the next project. If you are making the other parts as well, you will have to stay with it a bit longer.

GRATING

Whenever two or more ship model-makers are gathered together, you can bet that before long the conversation will get round to: 'How do you make your gratings?' There must be almost as many methods as there are modellers. At 1" to the foot scale the problem is fairly simple, as gratings are big enough to be made the proper way. Once you have made the simple jig required you can, should you so wish, turn out gratings by the mile (although for the life of me I cannot think why you should want to).

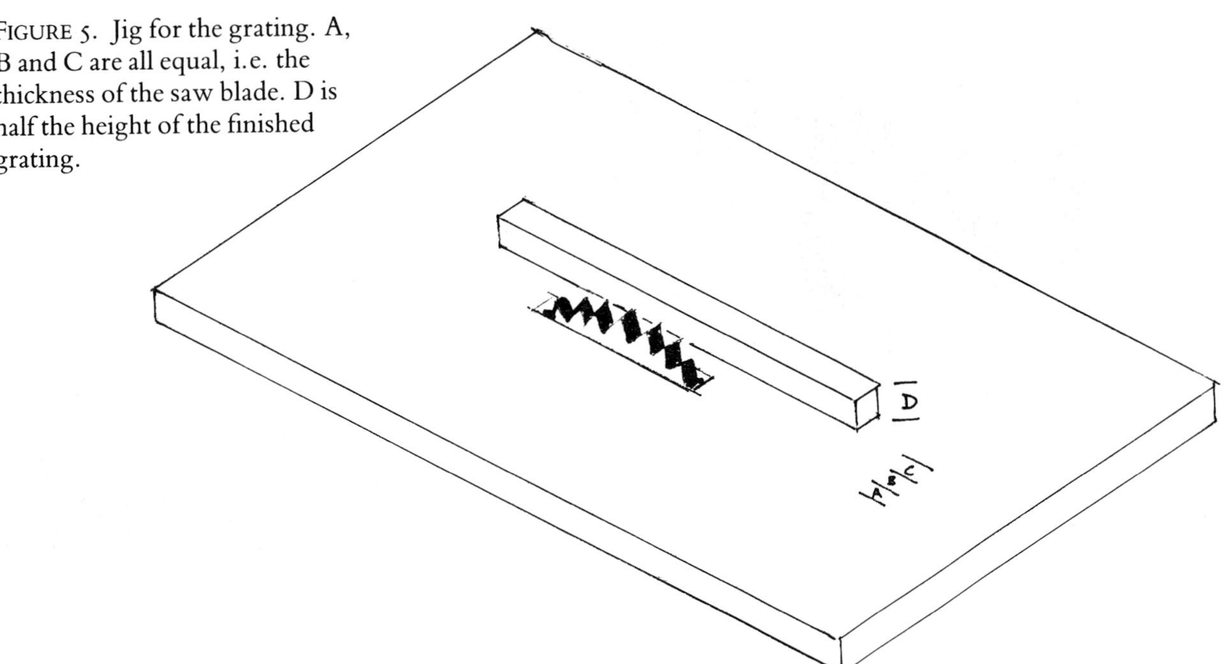

FIGURE 5. Jig for the grating. A, B and C are all equal, i.e. the thickness of the saw blade. D is half the height of the finished grating.

To make the jig, the first requirement is a circular saw of some kind, the blade of which should ideally be $\frac{1}{12}''$ thick. I have never seen a grating with holes bigger than 2″ across, so your saw blade should be no thicker than $\frac{1}{6}''$ at the very most (the thickness of the saw blade determines the size of the grating). Most circular saws have a removable plate which the blade sticks up through, and it is this plate which needs to be either modified or replaced. If possible, replace it, as most saws have far too much space between the blade and the plate. I like to use perspex for the jig, as it is easy to work and very easy to weld together with the right adhesive. (Ether is a bit old hat nowadays, apart from being very dangerous.)

Prepare a new top plate, and fix the saw on with the blade as low as possible. The timber for the grating needs to be $\frac{3}{16}''$ thick, and your saw blade should project half that again above the new plate, i.e. $\frac{3}{32}''$. Glue a strip $\frac{3}{32}''$ high and of the same width as the saw blade to either one side or the other, and at a distance away also equal to the width of the saw blade – see Figure 5. In practice you will find that both dimensions of the strip will have to be a shade under to allow the timber to slide easily.

PHOTOGRAPH 6. The pieces for making the grating.

To make a grating, pass a prepared piece of wood across the saw. This will cut a groove in the wood. Next, slot the groove over the perspex strip and pass the wood across the saw again, and so on until you have enough grooves, as in Photograph 6. In order to do this you will have to remove the riving knife from the saw blade. This is, of course, something you should never do, and to get away with it you must remember the golden rule that applies when using any machine tool: CONCENTRATE ALL THE TIME, for as sure as you are reading this, if you start getting blasé or careless, THE MACHINE WILL HAVE YOU, and even $\frac{3}{32}''$ of circular saw blade can make a nasty mess of your fingers.

All that remains is to slice the grooved timber into strips, again of the same width as the saw blade. Fit them together, like an old-fashioned egg-box, to the required size, glue an edging round, and there you have an excellent grating.

TELEMOTOR

Two further items need to be made if you are going to copy the example in the photographs. The first is the telemotor stand to hang the wheel from, and the second is something

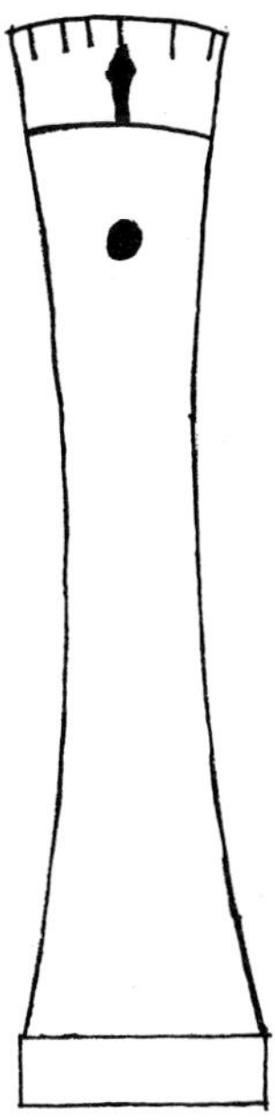

FIGURE 6a. Front elevation of telemotor stand, circular on plan.

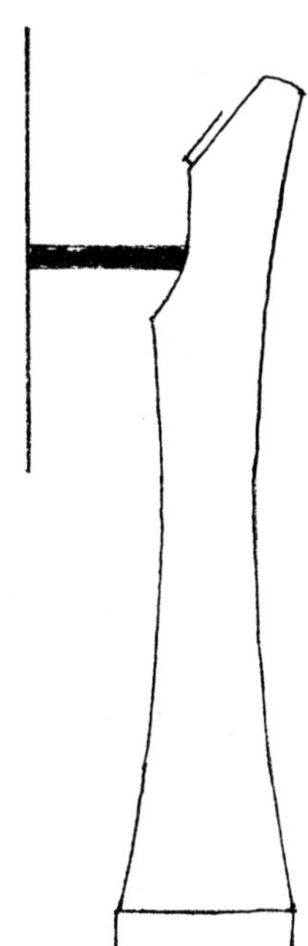

FIGURE 6b. Side elevation of telemotor stand.

to put the telemotor stand on. The telemotor stand is very easy and can be copied from Figures 6a and b. On the front is a brass plate with a pointer to indicate how much wheel is on. If you really want to be superior, you can make the gearing necessary for this feature to work – mine does not.

DECK

The deck section consists of 4″ scale planks made of oak. Cut enough strips of oak to cover the area, hold them all together and glue black paper to one edge (this is to represent the pitch seams between planks). As with most things connected with ship-building, there are rules governing the way that deck planking is laid. With just a small section being laid, the only rule of interest is the one concerning something called 'shift of butts'. This says that butt joints in the run of a plank shall not appear on the same line in adjacent planks. Photograph 6 shows the deck, which has a three plank shift, i.e. there are three whole planks between adjacent butted ones. Lay and glue the planks on a base, with due regard for the spacing of the butts. Drill each plank at intervals and glue in a dowel (cocktail sticks will do very well). Clean the piece off, seal and polish it. Fix the telemotor stand and secure the wheel. If you wish, you can complete the appearance of the edge of the deck area with a hockey stick moulding.

PHOTOGRAPH 7. Layout of the deck section showing shift of butts.

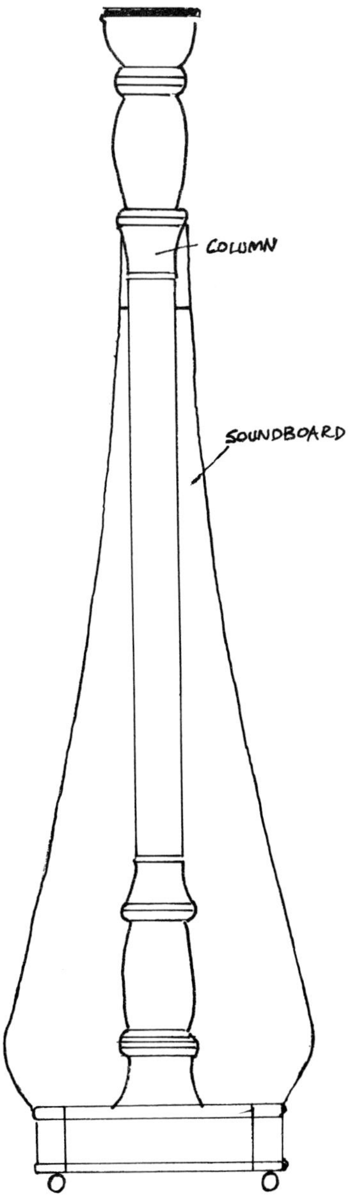

MODERN ORCHESTRAL HARP

FIGURE 1.

IN THE nineteenth century, harps were much more ornate than they are today, the column being richly decorated and the soundboard inlaid. This model is of a modern harp, but the general principles are exactly the same, so you can increase the decoration without having to alter any of the principal dimensions from the drawings.

To make the plain lines of this harp a little more interesting, the column, base and neck are made from Indian rosewood. The soundboard is made of ash, and the body of pine with a birdseye maple veneer.

COLUMN

Starting with the column, this needs to be turned to the shape in Figure 1. (Sharp-eyed readers will observe that the drawing and the photographs do not exactly agree. This is because my lathe will not take a piece of wood quite long enough to make the column in one length. The drawing shows a column which *is* turned from one length.) If you do decide to make the column from rosewood, be warned that it is a messy wood to work, and the dust may affect some people, so it is as well to wear a mask.

PHOTOGRAPH 1. The modern orchestral harp.

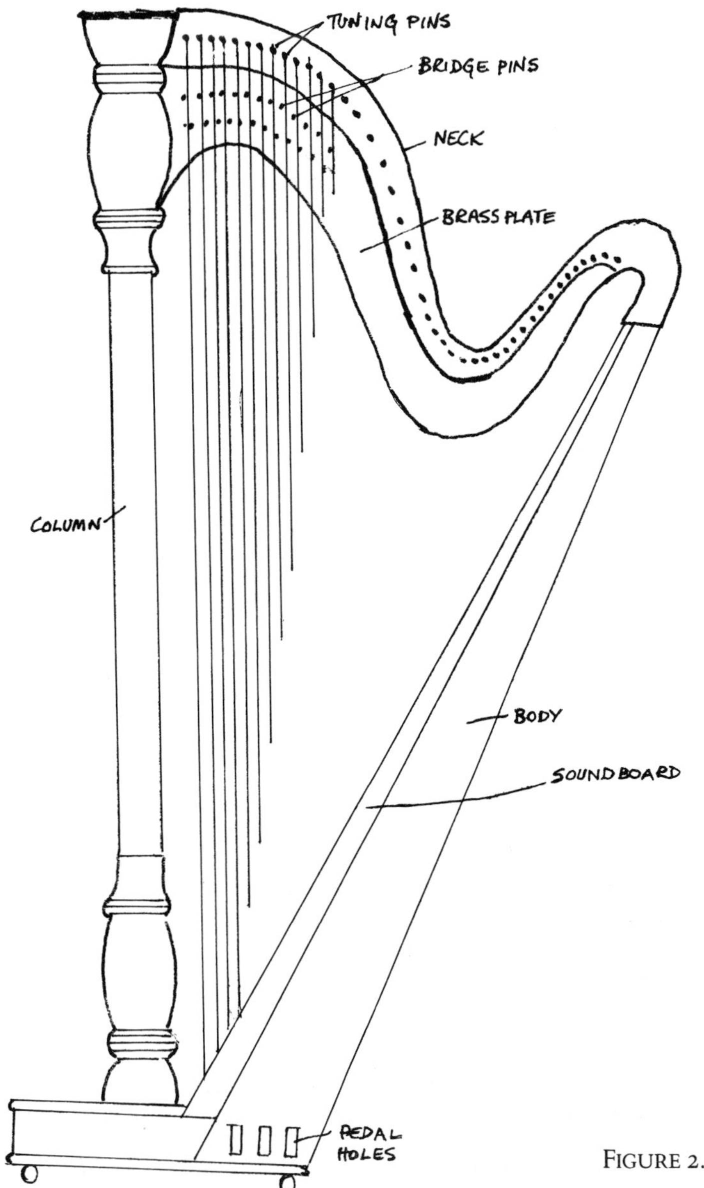

FIGURE 2.

NECK

Turn and polish the column before removing it from the lathe.

The next step is to mark and cut out the neck. As this is

only half the thickness of the top of the soundboard, it is necessary to add a small doubling piece to the soundboard end of the neck, but leave the final shaping until the harp is put together. The neck needs to be let into the top of the column just enough for there to be a flat surface upon which the neck can be fixed. At this stage do not glue the neck to the column as it is much easier to fix the brass plate and drill the neck for the tuning-pins before putting the whole assembly together.

FIGURE 3. Rear top section showing offset of neck.

FIGURE 4. Sketch showing offset of neck.

The brass plate has many movable bridge-pins which work from the pedals in the base and alter the pitch of the strings. They must of course be represented, but the added complications of actually stringing the harp persuaded me to content myself with a representation only. Cut out the brass plate (from Figure 2) and on the reverse mark with a centre punch, lightly, some eighty dots. When the plate is glued to the neck, these will appear as little pips. Reasonable, but obviously not as realistic as pins – perhaps next time!

Fix the brass plate to the neck, and then drill the neck for the tuning-pins. Use ordinary dressmaking pins for these and drill accordingly. Most harps seem to have between 40 and 48 strings – the one in the photographs has 42.

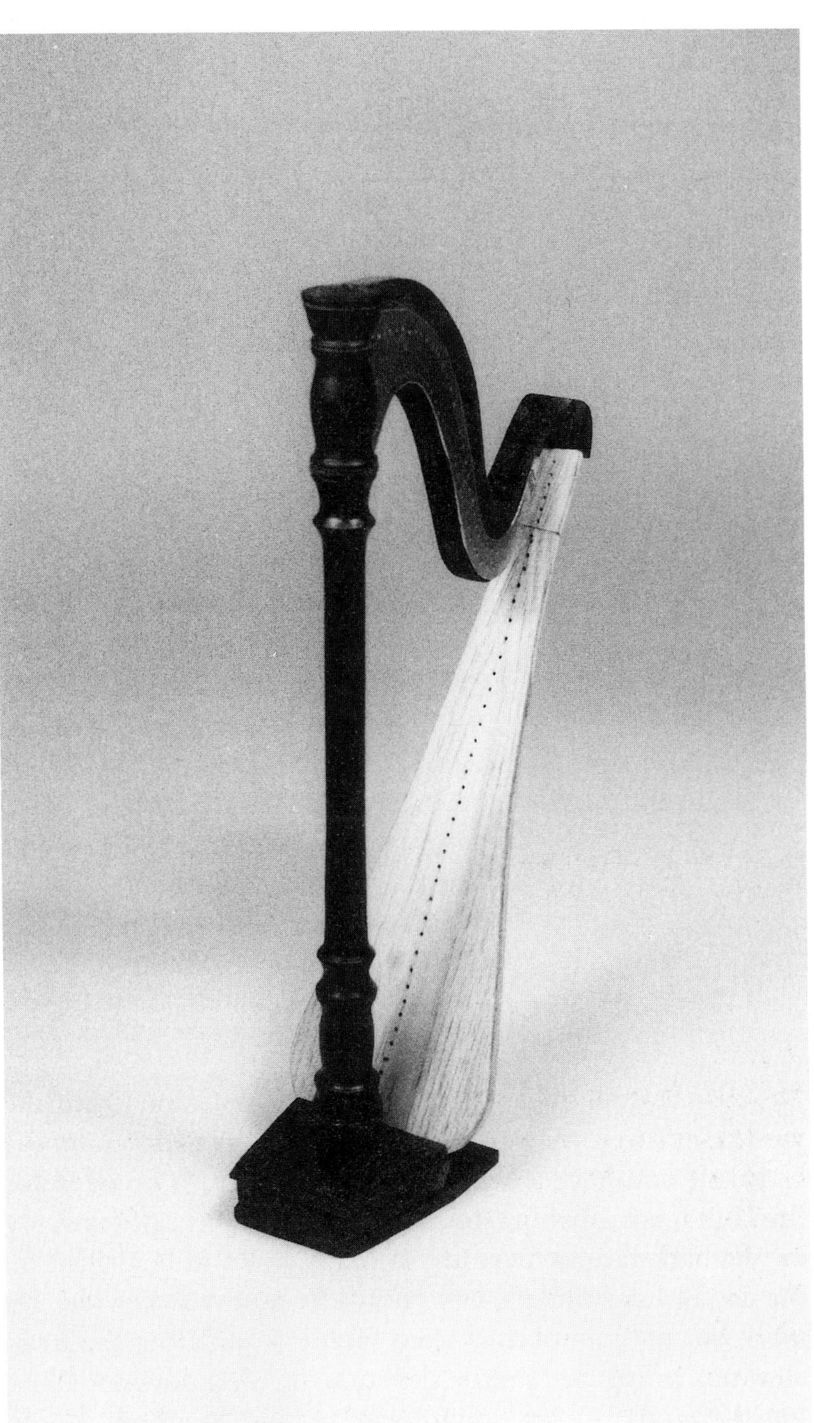

PHOTOGRAPH 2. The harp ready for stringing.

BASE

Still before gluing anything together, make the base. It is best to use three separate pieces for this, because it makes it considerably easier to achieve the raked angles caused by the soundboard and body joining the base at an oblique angle. The bottom piece (Figure 5) can be marked and cut direct from the drawing. The middle section stops short to allow the body to sit on the bottom piece (see Figure 2). The top section stops even shorter to allow the soundboard to sit on the middle section (again see Figure 2). Form a round, ovolo, or cove on the edge of the top section to finish it, and glue the three parts together.

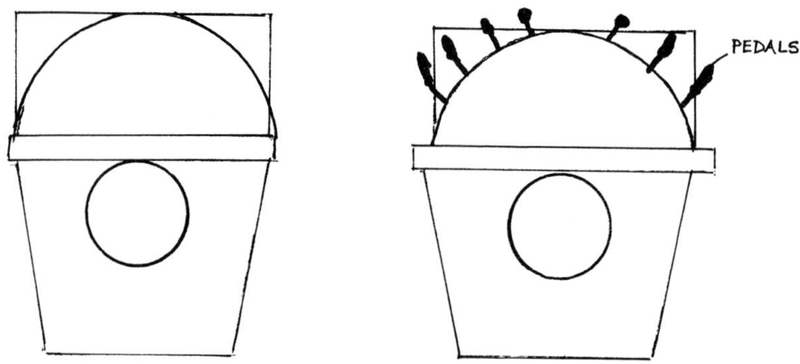

FIGURE 5. Plan of base plate.

SOUNDBOARD

Next is the soundboard (Figure 6). My ash came from the garden, and as it was not quite wide enough I had to joint the board. If you have a big enough piece, there is no need for this, but it is probably a good idea to glue a piece of 1mm ply on the back face as there are so many holes to be drilled on the centre line. The ply only needs to be about $\frac{1}{4}$″ wide. *Do* mark out the soundboard from Figure 6, not from the front elevation in Figure 1, as the elevation drawing does not allow for the angle. (Your soundboard would be about $\frac{1}{2}$″ too short, provoking much swearing!) Finally, drill along the centre line for the strings, see Photograph 2.

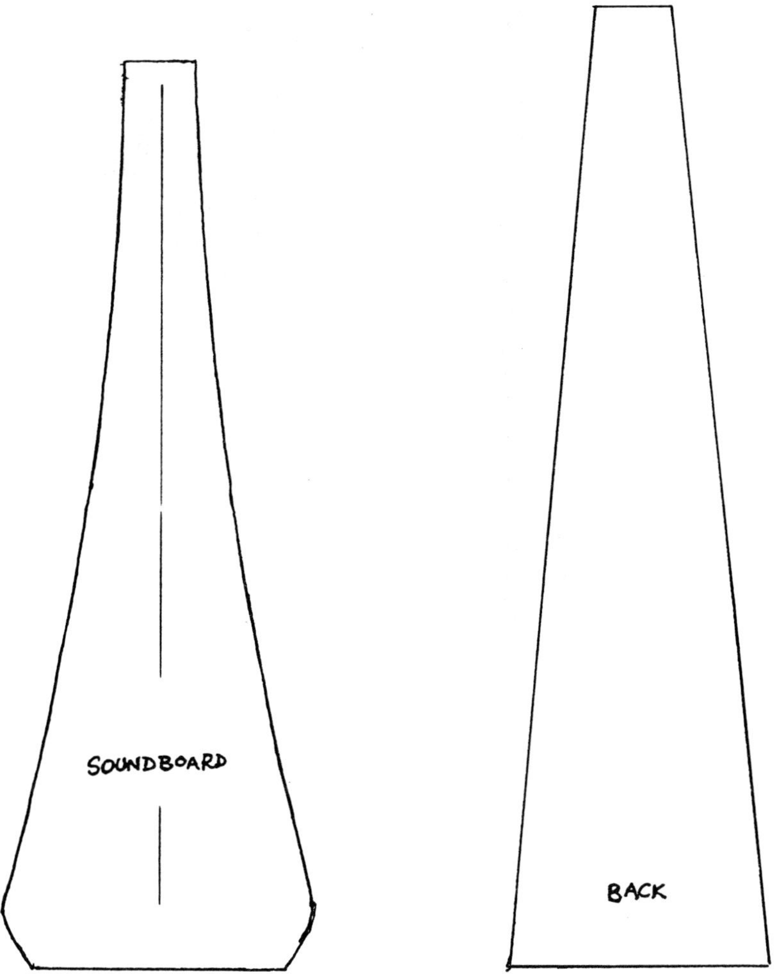

FIGURE 6. Expansion drawing of the back of the soundboard.

BODY

The body of my harp was made from pine and then veneered. The thinking behind this was that the pine would be easier to turn, and I also wanted to use birdseye maple, which is almost impossible to obtain other than as a veneer. (If birdseye does not look as good as you hoped, you will probably find it just as easy to turn the body from the

PHOTOGRAPH 3. The body and the soundboard in more detail.

finished wood of your choice – beech, perhaps?) The body is a gentle taper from the top width of the soundboard to the middle section of the base. It does not follow the extreme width of the soundboard which, when viewed from the back, projects on either side of the body. When you are happy with the turning, remove it from the lathe and cut it in half. Hollow it along the centre line of the straight side to allow the strings to fit in.

PHOTOGRAPH 4. Front elevation.

ASSEMBLY AND STRINGING

Now the main framework can be put together. This is another of those occasions when three hands would be a great advantage, but a dowel in the bottom of the column will help, and gluing the neck to the column and letting it set first will also make life easier. With a bit of luck all the bits will go together as they should with a minimum of fitting. At this stage *do not* attempt to glue the body in place – the stringing must be done first. I will admit that the first one I made took eight hours just to string, but that did include working out the easiest way to do it, so that you, gentle reader, should be able to do it rather more quickly.

The first thing to do is insert all the pins in the neck, cutting them so that about ⅛″ projects. Next, take your stringing material (and here I would suggest that wire is by far the easiest thing to use, and an appropriate size can be found in an old transformer or electric motor) and tie one end to the tuning-pin with a simple overhand knot. Thread the other end through the soundboard and twist it around one of the spare pins towards the outside of the back of the soundboard. Continue with this for the forty-odd pins,

PHOTOGRAPH 5. The pins tied off at the back of the soundboard.

adding tying-off pins to the back of the soundboard as necessary. Try to get the wires just tight enough to make them lie straight – too much tension and you may find that you have bowed the soundboard, and then you will have trouble getting the body to fit.

When all the strings are in, put a spot of glue on each of the pins. Ensure that all the strings are reasonably ten sioned and run a line of epoxy glue along the back of the soundboard to fix them. When cured, remove the tying-off pins and cut the wires short.

FINISHING

The body can now be fitted and glued to the back of the soundboard. The strings and line of glue will fit snugly into the groove in the body. To complete, drill and fit the representation of the pedals to the back of the body, and finish with the necessary polish. You may find that the harp is very finely balanced, in which case a hole drilled in the front of the base and some lead tapped in will cure the problem.

MEASURING NEW PROJECTS

I HOPE that having tried at least one or two of the preceding projects, you will have been bitten by the miniature bug and will want to make some original models of your own. I would guess that some of you will be saying, 'It's all right for him, but I could never measure something and produce drawings.' My answer to this is that following the method I have been using for years, it is really not nearly as difficult as you imagine. As long as you have the use of a camera, and can manage to point it at the object from which you would like to make the miniature, you are in business.

The photographs from which the drawings of the harp in this book are taken. The measuring stick is clearly visible!

MEASURING STICK

One other thing you will need is a measuring stick. The one I use is a single length of five feet, but a metre one will do. (In fact it does not even have to be a proper measuring stick – any straight stick will do, provided that you mark it out accurately.)

The marking out is also not difficult, and only has to be done once. Mine is a dark-coloured stick, and was already marked in inches. I put a length of 1″ white masking tape over the width of the stick at every alternate inch, so that the inches were alternately light and dark, as shown in the photographs.

SCALING DOWN

You are now ready to measure your chosen object, but please remember that if the piece of furniture or whatever does not belong to you, you should ask permission to measure it from the owner. I always request this either at the time or, better still, in advance, in writing. I can honestly say that I have never received anything but courtesy and co-operation.

What you must do is take a photograph, or series of photographs, of the object, with the measuring stick prominently displayed next to it, the stick being kept, as far as possible, either vertical or horizontal. The only other important point is to keep the camera as nearly square to the object as you can. If you start getting acute angles, the measurements will also become a bit inaccurate. Before leaving, take a few check measurements with a rule. For example, with the harp I took the overall height, width, and maximum and minimum dimensions of the soundboard.

When the photographs have been developed and printed, you will find that you can do your drawing quite easily by taking all the dimensions from them. It does not matter what size they have been enlarged to, as on each photograph there is a scale. You know that each light or dark section represents an inch, so it is easy to make a small-scale section on the edge of a postcard and take off the required measurement. Indeed, if I am working just for myself, I do not always bother to do a drawing, but work straight from the photographs.

One last point: to be as accurate as possible, always take your scale section from the point of the stick nearest to the part you wish to measure.

HAPPY MINIATURING

One final thought before we part company. I firmly believe that all modelling is a form of art, and that in making a miniature, sometimes the secret is knowing what to leave out. Too much detail can produce a miniature that is far more fussy than the original. A better guide at times is:

IF IT LOOKS RIGHT, THEN IT PROBABLY IS.

Happy miniaturing.